The Atonement

MARTIN HENGEL

The Atonement

**The Origins of the Doctrine
in the New Testament**

FORTRESS PRESS   PHILADELPHIA

Translated by John Bowden from an extended article, *Der stellvertretende Sühnetod Jesu. Ein Beitrag zur Entstehung des urchristlichen Kerygmas*, first published in German in the *Internationale katholische Zeitschrift 9*, 1980, 1–25, 135–47, with substantial additions by the author.

First British Edition by SCM Press Ltd. 1981

First American Edition by Fortress Press 1981

• **Library of Congress Cataloging in Publication Data**

Hengel, Martin.
    The atonement.

    "Translated by John Bowden from an extended
article, Der stellvertretende Sühnetod Jesu: ein
Beitrag zur Entstehung des urchristlichen Kerygmas,
first published in German in the Internationale
katholische Zeitschrift 9, 1980, 1–25, 135–47,
with substantial additions by the author"—Verso
of t.p.
    Bibliography: p.
    Includes indexes.
    1. Atonement—Biblical teaching. 2. Atonement.
3. Bible. N.T.—Criticism, interpretation, etc.
I. Title.
BS2545.A8H46 1981   232'.3   80–2384
ISBN 0–8006–1446–1   AACR2

8574A81 Printed in the United States of America 1–1446

In memory of Joachim Jeremias
20 September 1900 – 6 September 1979

CONTENTS

ABBREVIATIONS

AGAJU	Arbeiten zur Geschichte des antiken Judentums und des Urchristentums, Leiden
AnBib	Analecta Biblica
ANTJ	Arbeiten um Neuen Testament und Judentum
ARW	*Archiv für Religionswissenschaft*
ATANT	Abhandlungen zur Theologie des Alten und Neuen Testaments
AzTh	Arbeiten zur Theologie
BEvTh	Beiträge zur evangelischen Theologie
BFCT	Beiträge zur Förderung christlicher Theologie
BWANT	Beiträge zur Wissenschaft vom Alten und Neuen Testament
CBQ	*Catholic Biblical Quarterly*
CC	Corpus Christianorum
ET	English translation
ETS	Erfurter theologische Studien
EvTh	*Evangelische Theologie*
FGrHist	Fragmente der griechischen Historiker, ed. F. Jacoby
FRLANT	Forschungen zur Religion und Literatur des Alten und Neuen Testaments
GRBS	*Greek, Roman and Byzantine Studies*
HAW	Handbuch der Altertumswissenschaft
HSCP	*Harvard Studies in Classical Philology*
HTK	Herders theologischer Kommentar zum Neuen Testament
HTR	*Harvard Theological Review*
JSHRZ	*Jüdische Schriften aus hellenistisch-römischer Zeit*
JTS	*Journal of Theological Studies*
KAT	Kommentar zum Alten Testament
KEK	Kritisch-exegetischer Kommentar über das Neue Testament, founded by Heinrich August Wilhelm Meyer
KlT	Kleine Texte
LAB	Liber Antiquitatum Biblicarum (Pseudo-Philo)
LCL	Loeb Classical Library
LXX	Septuagint (Greek text)
M	Massoretic (Hebrew) text

MBT	Münsterische Beiträge zur Theologie
MPL	J. P. Migne, *Patrologia, Series Latina*
NT.S	*Novum Testamentum* Supplement
NTA	Neutestamentliche Abhandlungen
NTS	*New Testament Studies*
OBO	Orbis biblicus et Orientalis
PFLUS	Publications de la faculté des lettres de l'université de Strasbourg
POx	Oxyrhynchus Papyri
PW	*Paulys Realencyclopädie der classischen Altertumswissenschaft*
QD	Quaestiones disputatae
RB	*Revue Biblique*
RBPH	*Revue belge de philologie et d'histoire*
REJ	*Revue des études juives*
RhMus	*Rheinisches Museum für Philologie*
RM	Religionen der Menschheit
RVV	Religionsgeschichtliche Versuche und Vorarbeiten
SAH	Sitzungsberichte der Heidelberger Akademie der Wissenschaften
SANT	Studien zum Alten und Neuen Testament
SBS	Stuttgarter Bibelstudien
SBT	Studies in Biblical Theology
SCHNT	Studia ad Corpus Hellenisticum Novi Testamenti
SIFC	*Studi Italiani di Filologia Classica*
SNVAO.HF	Skrifter utgitt av det norske videnskaps-akademi i Oslo. Historisk-filosofisk klasse
StNT	Studien zum Neuen Testament
StPB	Studia Post-biblica
SUNT	Studien zur Umwelt des Neuen Testament
SVF	*Stoicorum veterum fragmenta*
TBAW	Tübinger Beiträge zur Altertumswissenschaft
TDNT	*Theological Dictionary of the New Testament*
ThQ	*Theologische Quartalschrift*
TLZ	*Theologische Literaturzeitung*
TU	Texte und Untersuchungen zur Geschichte der altchristlichen Literatur
TZ	*Theologische Zeitschrift* (Basle)
WMANT	Wissenschaftliche Monographien zum Alten und Neuen Testament
WUNT	Wissenschaftliche Untersuchungen zum Neuen Testament
ZNW	*Zeitschrift für die neutestamentliche Wissenschaft und die Kunde der älteren Kirche*
ZThK	*Zeitschrift für Theologie und Kirche*

INTRODUCTION

This short study ultimately goes back to the T. W. Manson Memorial Lecture which I gave at Manchester University on 1 November 1979. That was published in the *Bulletin of the John Rylands Library* 62, 1980, 454–75. The original and more extensive German version appeared in the *Internationale katholische Zeitschrift* 9, 1980, 1–25, 135–47, but the work which is presented here in John Bowden's translation has been expanded yet further at almost every point and has also been provided with notes. In particular, I have completely rewritten the first part, which is concerned with the background to the subject in ancient religion. Like my earlier investigations, e.g. *The Son of God* and *Crucifixion*, this book is part of the prolegomena to a comprehensive *Christology of the New Testament*. Far more than has happened in the past, scholars need to associate christology with a history of earliest Christianity. The history of primitive Christianity is essentially the history of its christology. Furthermore, the particular characteristics of its historical development can only be described against the background of the history of religion and culture in the ancient world. I have therefore been concerned to investigate not only the main Jewish sources but also the linguistic and conceptual material available in the Graeco-Roman world. As generally understood, the distinction between 'Old Testament and Jewish' and 'Greek and Hellenistic', would seem to be highly questionable, because from the middle of the fourth century onwards the so-called 'Old Testament Jewish tradition' increasingly came under Greek influence, while from an early period down to Hellenistic times we find a number of Eastern and Semitic influences on the Greek world. Without doubt there are differences, but we must begin from the fact that in antiquity the world of the Eastern Mediterranean formed a relative unity. The real contrasts in cultural and religious development emerge only from a more detailed consideration.

In its present form, this work cannot be more than a fragment. The reason why I have nevertheless allowed it to be published in this form is that the situation in many German universities is fundamentally inimical to scholarly work: the burden of teaching, examining and administration no longer allows the university professor to produce large-scale, comprehensive monographs within a reasonable length of time. Those who are plagued by a chronic lack of time have to approach their goal one short step after another.

In the present theological situation, my hope is that this study will help readers to understand that intensive 'historical-critical' work on biblical sources and material from the world of antiquity need not in any way lead to an obscuring of the truth of the gospel; on the contrary, by working out patterns of speech in the ancient world and showing how the central statements of the earliest Christian message came into being, it will lead to a better understanding. Faith itself provides the stimulus towards acquiring a better understanding and therefore sets in motion historical investigation, which must always be critical. To alter Anselm's famous remark slightly, we might say that this is _fides quaerens veritatem historicam_.

I am grateful to Dr Hermann Lichtenberger for reading the proofs.

I have dedicated this book to the memory of Joachim Jeremias, the most significant New Testament scholar of the last generation in Germany. 'Atonement' was a crucial theme of his life's work. It is now almost a year since he died, on 6 September 1979. This year he would have been eighty years old. I hope he may find successors to carry on his work.

Tübingen,
July 1980

I

Preliminary Questions

(i) The problem

No human death has influenced and shaped the world of late antiquity, and indeed the history of mankind as a whole down to the present day, more than that of the Galilean craftsman and itinerant preacher who was crucified before the gates of Jerusalem in AD 30 as a rebel and messianic pretender. Thousands of men had been executed by crucifixion there by the Roman prefects and later procurators, in the sixty-five years, or thereabouts, between the transformation of Judaea into a Roman province and the end of the Jewish War. The internal Jewish tradition in the Talmudim and Midrashim has completely suppressed these countless victims of the Roman governing power down to the time of the destruction of the Second Temple. Josephus' work, preserved thanks to the Christian tradition, mentions a very few names, but apart from that, they have all been forgotten.[1] The fact that this one Galilean was not forgotten, but had a unique effect on world history, especially by means of his death, is connected with the way in which this death was interpreted: it became the foundation of Christian faith. In what follows, the most important question that we shall have to answer is: how did it come about that the disciples of Jesus could proclaim that cruel, disastrous execution of their master as the saving event *par excellence*? In other words, how did the crucifixion of Jesus come to take its place at the centre of early Christian preaching?[2] How was it that this infamous death could so quickly be interpreted as a representative, atoning, sacrificial death, and in what interpretative framework was such an understanding possible at all?

New Testament scholars usually attempt to come close to the basic event on which the Christian community was founded by means of form-critical and traditio-critical analyses of the earliest pieces of tradition that we have. We shall also have to adopt this approach in the following pages, but by itself it is not enough to provide an answer to our question. We shall have to understand that in a broader historical context.

As a result, I have to begin with a quite different, rather unusual question. How did the *Gentile audience* in the Graeco-Roman world understand this strange new message of the crucified and risen Son of God and Redeemer? Were its categories, for example that of the representative atoning death of Jesus, completely alien to people who did not know either the Old Testament or the Jewish Haggadah? Or, barbarous and offensive as the new doctrine of salvation must have seemed to the educated, did it not also contain basic concepts which were quite familiar to people in Ephesus, Corinth or Rome?

Another preliminary point should be made here. One of the most important historical distinctions with which New Testament scholarship has worked since the emergence of the history-of-religions school is the sharpest possible division between the 'Old Testament and Jewish' and the 'Hellenistic' tradition. This distinction became almost a tenet of faith for German scholarship, which divided 'conservative' from 'critical' theologians. Of course, over the last few years – slowly enough – the view has spread that this abrupt distinction is far too blurred, and indeed is sometimes positively misleading. The Jews of the time of Jesus and the apostles had been living for about four hundred years under the influence of Greek civilization, with its scientific and technical superiority, even in the mother country of Palestine, and in any case the world of late antiquity forms a relative cultural and spiritual unity, which moreover spoke a common, elementary religious *koinē*, spreading even beyond the linguistic barriers of the Semitic and Greek worlds. Only if we take this fact into account can we provide a historical explanation for phenomena like the origin of the Septuagint and the literature of Greek-speaking Judaism, which extended as far as Palestine itself, or the astonishing missionary success of the Jewish-messianic sect of the Christians which from its base in Judaea penetrated so rapidly into the Graeco-Roman world. The Jewish upper classes in Palestine were also largely bilingual, and the allegedly 'anti-Hellenistic' Pharisees and the rabbinate which developed from them after AD 70 were deeply influenced by their cultural environment. It would not be much of an exaggeration to describe the whole of Judaism in the Hellenistic Roman period as 'Hellenistic Judaism'. New Testament scholarship can no longer escape this recognition.[3]

Now of course it is strange that despite this growing insight, when it comes to the question of the origin of the soteriological interpretation of the death of Jesus the old dispute between 'Hellenists' and 'Judaizers' has flared up again in a new and acute way. Particularly in Germany during the last ten years, over against the more traditional view that the interpretation of the death of Jesus as a representative atoning death comes from Old Testament and Jewish sources, it has been argued with some emphasis that in the last resort the 'death of Jesus for us' is to be derived from Greek sources and was first developed in the Hellenistic (Jewish-Christian) community.[4] In contrast to that, there were supposed to be quite different earlier, typically Jewish, categories of interpretation, which could be traced back to the earliest Palestinian community, and perhaps even to the proclamation of Jesus himself: first, that prophets are killed by their own people, and secondly, that the righteous man is exalted to God only through suffering and death.[5] This conflict points to a real problem. If the tradition of the earliest, Aramaic-speaking, Jewish community in Palestine were thought to be solely responsible for the interpretation of the death of Jesus on the cross as an event bringing about salvation and atonement for the whole world, it would be hard to understand how this particular interpretation emerges so strongly in the 'missionary literature' of the New Testament which is addressed to Gentile Christians, for example the Pauline corpus, Hebrews and I Peter, whereas in the Palestinian tradition about Jesus to be found in the synoptic gospels it appears only in a very few places. In comparison with it, the tradition of the murder of the prophets is predominant in the Logia source (Q) and the theme of the 'suffering righteous' in the passion narrative. Of course we would immediately have to ask whether they are in fact so typically 'Jewish' or 'un-Hellenistic', and whether distinctions of this kind do not prove relatively unhelpful in understanding the New Testament texts.

(ii) The apotheosis of the dying hero

It is surely right that among the Greeks and Romans – to put it cautiously – a whole series of closer and more distant analogies can be found to the interpretation of the death of Jesus as a *presupposition for his exaltation* and also as a representative atoning death for others. This is also true not least of terminology, but it is not just limited to that. I shall begin with a number of well-known instances. We find a voluntary acceptance of death, as the way to divine honour indicated by the gods, in a number of places in Greek myth, and in particular in connection with its most prominent figures, above all the two most popular heroes of antiquity, Heracles and Achilles. 'While the pyre was burning, it is said that a cloud passed under Heracles and with a peal of thunder wafted him up to heaven',[6] whereas the son of Peleus decided to rush off into battle against Hector, despite the warning of his divine mother, in order to meet the murderer of his beloved friend: '. . . and then I myself will accept my fate, when Zeus and the other immortal gods resolve to bring it about'. A short but glorious life seemed more desirable than a long but inglorious one.[7] In the post-Homeric saga, Thetis carries aloft the corpse of her son; in Pindar he appears as the judge of the dead (*Olympian Odes* 2,77), while other poets transport him to Elysium or to the island of Leuke in the Black Sea, where he is venerated as a god and leads an immortal life. However, one could also point to historical figures, e.g. Empedocles. To some degree depending on the audience, the saga describes how he leapt into Etna to achieve his own apotheosis, or experienced a miraculous transportation by night (Diogenes Laertius 8.67f.). There is also Plato's account of the death of Socrates, which has quite a different form. Faithful to the inner command of the god, Socrates fulfilled his task in Athens and, mindful of the laws of the city, did not try to escape the unjust death penalty imposed on him, but fearlessly drank the cup of hemlock. In this way he becomes the prototype of the martyr who looks death fearlessly in the eye for the sake of the truth – in the last resort a divine truth – which he represents.[8] We might well ask whether the theme of the 'innocent sufferer', suffering for the truth of the law, which makes such an evocative appearance in the Hellenistic period, is as Jewish as all that. It may also be influenced decisively by the ideal of the martyred philosopher, which is substantially older than the specifically Jewish transfiguration of the death of the pious and the righteous. Any historical investigation which is to do justice to the New Testament cannot be content with stressing the tradition of the Old Testament and Judaism, important though that may be; it must also pay very close attention to the Graeco-Roman world, where the problems become particularly interesting at the point where Jewish and Greek conceptions have already become fused in the pre-Christian period. By the providence of God, the New Testament is written in Greek, and not Hebrew or Aramaic.

The ancient ideal of the *voluntary heroic apotheosis achieved through death* also appears in the person of the Cynic – and erstwhile Christian – Peregrinus Proteus, who immolated himself in Olympia in AD 165. The satirist Lucian described his life and death in a malicious account. He is said to have hurled himself on to the burning pyre with the cry 'May the gods of my mother and father be gracious to me', and as in the Romulus saga and the apotheosis of the Roman emperors, his transportation to heaven is confirmed by eyewitnesses (Lucian, *Peregrinus* 36.39f.). Parium, his home town, erected a statue of him which, according to the testimony of the Christian apologist Athenagoras (26), is said to have brought about miracles. Here Peregrinus followed the example of Heracles, the Indian Brahmans and the strict Cynic doctrine that death is on no account to be feared because it brings the liberation of the soul. In contrast to Lucian's caricature, many contemporaries seem to have thought highly of the philosopher for his strict standards: he did not hesitate to attack the emperor, the government and the mightiest men in the Empire, and as a result was banished from Rome.[9] The fact that according to Lucian, Peregrinus taught that he was dying 'for men's welfare' (ὑπὲρ τῶν ἀνθρώπων), to teach them to despise death and to overcome their fears (ἐγκαρτερεῖν τοῖς δεινοῖς, 23, cf. 33), might well suggest that he was parodying the attitudes of Christian martyrs.

These instances of voluntary death as the way towards deification could be supplemented by numerous legends about the transportation or ascension of the living and the dead to the gods: from Romulus and Alcmene through the legendary poet Aristeas, mentioned by Herodotus, to the transportation of Caesar and the later emperors and their apotheoses.[10]

(iii) Dying for the city and for friends

On the other hand, it is striking that while we have the transportation of two living men, Enoch and Elijah, in the Old Testament, there is no instance of the transportation of anyone who has died, much less of a numinous transfiguration of death or even of a divine glorification of the dead. In a radical way, which is unique in the ancient world, death is robbed of its religious autonomy in a way which makes the cult of the dead, widespread among mankind and particularly in the ancient world, quite impossible. One might almost say that the fact that the deceased ancestors in Israel ceased to be *autonomous* numinous beings was a revolutionary development. The exclusive revelation of God to his people does not allow any special cult of 'heroes'. True, there are rites of mourning regulated by law and custom, and on death a man joined the 'community of his fathers', but belief in Yahweh did not allow any kind of worship of the dead or any cultic or magical dealings with them. Whereever anything of this kind appears on the periphery – as with the witch of Endor (I Sam. 28) – it is condemned out of hand as a religious evil.[11]

It is all the more significant that in the Hellenistic period, probably under the influence of the spirit of the age, a degree of autonomy was restored to the realm of the dead, even in Palestine and Babylonia – albeit strictly governed by belief in Yahweh's omnipotence.

For this reason, the glorification or even the superhuman transfiguration of the martyr is completely alien to the Old Testament. It simply does not occur in ancient Israel. The martyrdom of the faithful becomes an independent problem only in the latest book of the Old Testament canon, the apocalypse Daniel (11.33ff.), which was written in 165 BC, about the time of the climax of the Maccabean revolt. This is only possible because at the end, to some degree as God's answer, there is a statement of the resurrection hope (12.2f.). For this reason, the literary form of the account of a martyrdom is unknown to the Old Testament texts, because it presupposes not only the resurrection hope, which overcomes death, but also a particular interest in the person of the martyr as a heroic witness, and also in his suffering. Our first examples, II Macc. 6; 7, were written by a Jew with Greek education, who was, however, familiar with Palestinian piety.[12] By contrast, in ancient Israel there are hardly any examples of dying for Israel, the Law or the sanctuary, which are stressed as heroic actions.[13] There was no room here for praise of 'the acts of the dead': the sole concern was for the glory of God: 'Not unto us, O Lord, not to us, but to thy name give glory' (Ps. 115.1). Whenever there is any mention of dying for God's sake, as in Ps. 44.22: 'Nay, for thy sake we are slain all the day long, and accounted as sheep for the slaughter', this is not done to celebrate those who are killed in this way, or to praise human bravery, but to accuse God, who refuses to help the innocent people:

> Rouse thyself! Why sleepest thou, O Lord?
> Awake! Do not cast us off for ever!
> Why dost thou hide thy face?
> Why dost thou forget our affliction and oppression?
> (Ps. 44.24f.)

Death, which for Greeks and Romans is so glorious on the battle-field, is without reservation God's judgment and mystery; even in the case of a Jonathan, the friend of David who is portrayed in such sympathetic terms, or so God-fearing a king as Josiah. The lament about the mysterious person who is 'pierced' (Zech. 12.10ff.), which is probably connected with the tradition of Josiah's death, conceals more than it reveals.[14] His death remains an insoluble riddle. Even the heroic end of Samson, the Hebrew Heracles, who takes vengeance on his enemies by his own death (Judg. 16.26–30), seems like an alien body in ancient Israel. True, there are some references to individual prophets who are killed (Jer. 26.20ff.; II Chron. 24.20ff.) or persecuted, along with the Deuteronomistic accusations of the murder of prophets in Israel (cf. Neh. 9.26) but there is no real report of a prophetic martyrdom, far less any hints of a 'theology of martyrdom'.[15] The theme of the murder of the prophets serves as a basis for God's judgment on his people; there is still no interest in the dying prophets themselves and in the circumstances of their death. The death or the suffering of the pious at the hand of the wicked is not yet an independent theme. Commemoration of the martyr prophets and the legends associated with them (even including the veneration of their tombs) only begins to become more prominent in Palestine in the Hellenistic period. This was prompted, as far as I can see, by veneration of the tombs of Greek heroes.

A representative death to atone for the guilt of others can therefore be found at best on the periphery of the Old Testament – for example in Isa. 53, which K. Koch rightly describes as an 'erratic block'.[16] There is a good deal of argument about the interpretation and influence of this text even now, which we shall have to consider later (see pp. 57ff. below). As a rule, the possibility of such representation is rejected out of hand, since 'a person may die only for his own sins'.[17] Moses' request to God to forgive the sins of his people or to be able to die for them is expressly rejected by God himself: 'I blot out from my book only those who have sinned against me.'[18]

Again, we find examples of heroic 'dying for the people or for the Law' only in the Hellenistic period, above all after the time of the Maccabean rebellion. In I Maccabees, which was originally written in Hebrew, Mattathias admonishes his sons: 'Show zeal for the Law, and give your lives for (ὑπέρ) the covenant of our fathers.' The theme of glory appears a little later: 'And receive great honour and an everlasting name.'[19] Josephus presents this invitation in an even more Graecized version: 'So prepare your souls, so that, if necessary, you can die for the Law'; here he is clearly making use of a Greek formula known since Aristotle.[20] Subsequently, similar assertions can often be found in the mouth of Jewish martyrs and freedom fighters within Jewish Hellenistic writing.[21] The description of the heroic act of Eleazar, one of the Maccabee brothers, who killed a Seleucid elephant and was crushed by the beast's fall, is typical of the new, thoroughly Greek-sounding understanding of heroic death: 'He supposed that the king was upon it. So he gave his life to save his people and to win for himself an everlasting name.'[22] We shall have to return to this and other Jewish texts on a number of further occasions. At this point, however, it should already be noted that the Old Testament background is not enough to explain it.

The situation among the *Greeks* is quite different. For them, from the classical period onwards, ἀποθνῄσκειν ὑπέρ and more rarely also (ἐπι)διδόναι ἑαυτὸν ὑπέρ, or similar formulae with περί or πρό, so familiar from New Testament christological formulae, were a stereotyped expression for the voluntary sacrifice of a man's life in the interests of his *native city, his friends, his family* or – quite peripherally – also philosophical truth. Since this terminology, so far as I can see, has hardly been investigated at all in existing literature, I must dwell on it somewhat longer. The following study makes no claim to completeness. Rather, it has the character of a compilation of the fruits of relatively chance reading.

To deal with the phenomenon, a composite verb ὑπεραπο-θνῄσκειν was even formed. We find its content presented in an overwhelming way in Euripides' *Alcestis*, where Alcestis is pre-pared to die for her husband Admetus, whereas his old parents refuse to perform this service,[23] or in the *Phoenissae*, where Creon's son Menoeceus is ready to sacrifice himself for his country against his father's will. Creon wants 'to die as an atoning sacrifice for the city',[24] but his son sets off secretly: 'I am going, and will deliver the city, and I will give up my life to die for this land' (εἶμι καὶ σώσω πόλιν ψυχήν τε δώσω τῆσδ' ὑπερθανεῖν χθονός).[25] The re-solve of Heracles' daughter Macaria in the *Heraclides* is very much the same: she is prepared to sacrifice herself to save her kinsfolk: 'I voluntarily give my life for them, not under compulsion.'[26] In Plato's *Symposium*, dying for the beloved is stressed as a special

expression of the unique power of Eros (179B ff.: καὶ μὴν ὑπεραπο-
θνῄσκειν γε μόνοι ἐθέλουσιν οἱ ἐρῶντες).[27]
From the classical period onwards there are virtually innumer-
able statements which praise vicarious death in battle for the city.
In essentials, the idea itself goes back to Homer. Hector himself
urges on the Trojans:

> Go, fight at the ships in close groups,
> and if any of you, wounded by arrow or sword, should meet
>   death and fate,
> let him lie in death; it is no disgrace to die fighting for one's
>   country.
> (οὐ οἱ ἀεικὲς ἀμυνομένῳ περὶ πάτρης/τεθνάμεν)

We hear a very similar note from the Spartan poet Tyrtaeus:

> For it is honourable to be killed, to fall in battle among the
> foremost fighters as a brave man, for one's country.
> (τεθνάμεναι γὰρ καλὸν ἐνὶ προμάχοισι πεσόντα
> ἄδρ' ἀγαθὸν περὶ ᾗ πατρίδι μαρνάμενον)

Round about the same time the Ephesian Callinus wrote:

> For it is a glorious and honourable thing when a man fights
> for his country, his children and his wife.[28]
> (. . . ἀνδρὶ μάχεσθαι γῆς περί)

After the time of the Persian wars, the fame of dead heroes was
written on numerous honorific inscriptions and epitaphs for all to
see. From the many examples let me mention just one of the
earliest pieces of evidence, the memorial in Locrian Opus to those
who fell at Thermopylae:

> τούσδε ποτὲ φθιμένους ὑπὲρ Ἑλλάδος ἀντία Μήδων
> μητρόπολις Λοκρῶν εὐθυνόμων Ὀπόεις.
> Opus, metropolis of the Locrians of righteous laws,
> mourns for these who perished in defence of Greece against
>   the Medes.[29]

In the *Menexenus*, Plato's Socrates calls this praise of those who
have fallen for the city, 'who have accepted death in exchange for
the salvation of the living', both an appropriate praise of the fathers

and also a legitimate piece of self-esteem.[30] Pindar could celebrate dying for the city unequivocally as a religious sacrifice:

> Hearken, O war-shoot, daughter of war! Prelude of spears!
> To whom soldiers are sacrificed for their city's sake,
> In the holy sacrifice of death.
> (... ᾇ θύεται ἄνδρες ὑπὲρ πόλιος τὸν ἱερόθυτον θάνατον).[31]

Most recently, J. Gnilka has wanted to brush aside this wide-ranging evidence with its religious implications by observing that here 'the death which is died for others saves them exclusively from physical and material distress', or that 'the fame and reputation of the cause or institution under attack will be increased in an earthly and public context', and then goes on to conclude that 'these texts do not have any kind of theological significance'.[32] However, here he completely misunderstands the nature of ancient religion. It is taken for granted that dying for one's native city, its gods, holy laws and temples, for the tombs of dead ancestors and families, always also has an essentially religious character, and those who have fallen in battle for these supreme goods are worshipped as heroes, i.e. as divine beings. Even in Plutarch's time (about AD 100), those who fell at Plataea (478 BC) had sacrifices offered to them year by year as those 'who had died for the freedom of Greece', and the souls of the dead were summoned to taste the sacrificial blood.[33] The encomium of Simonides of Ceos at the celebration for all those who died at Thermopylae similarly expresses a deep religious sensibility:

> ... glorious is their destiny, fair their fate; *for an altar they have a tomb*, for libations remembrance, for wine mourning. No decay, no all-vanquishing time will deface this shrine of brave men, and the glory of Greece has made its abode in this hallowed precinct.[34]

Making heroes of those who had died in the Greek fight for freedom against the Persians introduced a new development. This is also connected with the fact that the unexpected victory over the Great King and the repulse of the Persian yoke was celebrated as a historical saving event, which more than any other historical event formed the basis for a general sense of being Greek which transcended all internal political differences.[35] In retrospect, it was explained more and more in religious terms; from now on other warriors, benefactors and saviours of cities were elevated and became demigods.[36] In this context there was a predilection for stressing that the dead had died not just for an individual *polis* but 'for Greece'. This is the case in the legendary answer of Leonidas, in which he rejected Xerxes' offer of shared rule over Greece: 'Death for Greece (ὁ ὑπὲρ τῆς Ἑλλάδος θάνατος) seems to me better than sole rule over my fellow countrymen.' His death was seen as a heroic sacrificial death for all Greece, in a deliberate parallel to the death of king Codrus (see below, pp. 13f.), and other figures from the mythical primal period. This model may even have influenced the motif of sacrifice in the plays of Euripides; at the same time it comes close to the Roman *devotio*.[37]

Of course the theme of 'dying for the fatherland' took on its greatest significance in political rhetoric. It appears for the first time in Thucydides in the famous speech of Pericles in honour of those who fell in the first year of the war, 431: 'who made the finest sacrifice for the city. For together they yielded up their bodies, and in return each received praise which does not grow old . . .'[38] We have a similar-sounding formula in the story of the three men in the burning fiery furnace, Dan. 3.28: 'They yielded up their bodies rather than serve and worship any god except their own God,' which is probably an indication that even in the early Hellenistic periods this 'surrender formula' had also found its way into Aramaic-speaking Judaism.[39]

Isocrates' *Panegyric*, which is fond of this formula, says that the fallen 'counted it worse to incur shame with their (fellow) citizens than to die in the right way for the city' (ἢ καλῶς ὑπὲρ τῆς πόλεως ἀποθνῄσκειν).[40] We also find similar statements somewhat less frequently in other Attic orators,[41] and not infrequently with later authors.[42] According to Cicero, the question '*Honestumne sit pro patria mori?*' is a rhetorical exercise.[43] Even in the *Acta Appiani*, which come from the sphere of the Alexandrian Acts of Martyrs, belonging to the time of Commodus, Heliodorus encourages the gymnasiarch Appian, whom the emperor has condemned to death, as he is led out to execution: 'Go, my son, die! It will bring you fame to die for a fatherland which is so sweet. Do not be afraid!' (τρέχε, τέκνον, τελεύτα. κλέος σοί ἐστιν ὑπὲρ τῆς γλυκυτάτης σου πατρίδος τελευτῆσαι. μὴ ἀγωνία).[44]

Obviously, dying for the *polis* was also included in the philosophers' catalogues of duties. Plato's *Menexenus* is dominated by this theme (see above, p. 10); in his *Nicomachean Ethics*, Aristotle associated the obligation to die for one's native city with giving up one's life, if necessary, 'for one's friends'. This extension of the *patris* to friends also indicates a loosening of the ties of the city which were supplemented – or even replaced – by the philosophical bond of friendship. E. Schwartz comments: 'Where the state can no longer be the foundation for a common ethic, voluntary φιλία insinuates itself'. This tendency is continued in the Hellenistic period. The Stoics after Chrysippus said that to sacrifice one's life for one's country or for one's friends was foremost among the reasons which justified one's voluntary death. On the other hand, for Epicurus and his followers, who were averse to all political activities, it was the mark of the wise man only 'in some circumstances to die for a friend'. Epictetus, too, limits himself to dying for friends.[45] This requirement is close to John 15.13 and Paul's remark in Rom. 5.6. However, for Paul, that the Son accepted death for God's *enemies* (Rom. 5.5–10) was a quite incomparable event.

By contrast the Cynics, who saw themselves as citizens of the world, rejected dying for institutions, along with dying for the state, war and the family, though – as the example of Peregrinus Proteus shows – they called for utter contempt of death.[46]

Romans and Greeks were familiar from childhood onwards with this ideal of representative dying for the community, as expressed in Horace's well-known and much misused verse '*dulce et decorum est pro patria mori*'.[47] This was one of the basic lessons of the ancient school. An exceptional instance of this 'dying for one's country' was the *voluntary self-sacrifice of a select individual* in the sense of 'one for all', e.g. the king or the general. Ancient texts relatively often mention the heroic example of Codrus, the legendary last king of Athens, who on the basis of an oracle went out to meet the enemy alone in slave's clothing; unrecognized, he was killed by them and in so doing saved Athens.[48] It was a favourite practice to cite the names of such heroes in rhetorical lists of examples. Cicero begins such a list with the comment: 'A noble death sought willingly for one's country is thought by orators not only to be praiseworthy but also to be happy' (*Clarae vero mortes pro patria oppetitae non solum gloriosae rhetoribus sed etiam beatae videri solent*). Even Vercingetorix delivered himself up to the Romans in order to spare his people,[49] and the emperor Otho, who had come to power in a somewhat disreputable way, displayed the ancient Roman attitude after receiving news of his defeat against Vitellius: 'Go to the victor and pay homage to him. I myself will free me from myself, that through this action, too, all men may learn that you have chosen the kind of emperor who not only sacrifices you for himself, but also sacrifices himself for you' (ὅστις οὐχ ὑμᾶς ὑπὲρ ἑαυτοῦ ἀλλ' ἑαυτὸν ὑπὲρ ὑμῶν δέδωκε). Despite the refusal of the soldiers, 'but we will all die *for you*', he killed himself. Dio Cassius cannot avoid praising him for this: 'after he had lived the most wicked of all men, he died in the most noble way'.[50]

The relatively well-educated conservative Christian Clement of Rome uses this theme of the sacrifice of an individual hero for the whole people in order to move the refractory Corinthians, as far as possible, to depart in the interest of peace in the community: 'Many kings and rulers, when a time of pestilence has set in, have followed the counsel of oracles, and given themselves up to death, that they might rescue their subjects through their own blood.' He probably has in mind here the ancient Roman custom of the *devotio* of the general, or is thinking of the kind of lists that we have in Cicero and other orators. As a biblical Jewish counterpart, Clement mentions Judith, who 'gave herself up to danger . . . for love of her country and her people in their siege',[51] i.e. a Jewish *Novelle* of the Maccabean period, which has typically Hellenistic features.

This theme is given a christological turn in the 'prophecy' of the high priest Caiaphas (John 11.50) that it is better 'that one man should die for the people, and that the whole nation should not perish'. In the archaic *devotio* already mentioned, the general dedicated himself or others to the gods of the underworld with the aim of also delivering his opponents over to the underworld by means of his own sacrificial death. If he then escaped with his life, for the rest of his life he was regarded as *impius*. The underlying idea of the *unum pro multis dabitur caput*[52] could also be formulated as a rabbinic rule: 'It is better that this man should be killed than that the community should be punished for his sake.'[53] Among the Christian church fathers after Clement of Alexandria, the classical Greek concept of ὑπεραποθνήσκειν was then transferred to the atoning death of Jesus, whereas Celsus reproaches the disciples of Jesus for 'neither dying with him nor for him', but denying him.[54]

(iv) Dying for the law and for truth

Voluntary death for the common good of one's city or one's friends *could also be transferred to spiritual ends.* Only through this transference did there come into being the real 'idea of the martyr', which then at a later stage became very significant in Judaism and even more so in Christianity. After all that has already been said, I need not stress further that it, too, is clearly Greek in origin. We already find a beginning of the transference of readiness to fight (and to die) for one's homeland into the spiritual sphere in the fine saying of Heraclitus: 'The people must fight for the law as for the wall' (μάχεσθαι χρὴ τὸν δῆμον ὑπὲρ τοῦ νόμου ὅκωσπερ τείχεος). εὐνομία to some degree formed the spiritual and social wall of a city, which in many circumstances protected it even against its own citizens. In the last resort, it is not human, but divine in origin: 'All human laws draw their sustenance from the one divine law.' For that very reason the νόμος calls for the sacrifice of all one's life.[55] Demosthenes finds it terrifying that the ancestors of the Athenians 'dared to die, so that the laws would not be destroyed' (προγόνους ὑπὲρ τοῦ μὴ καταλυθῆναι τοὺς νόμους ἀποθνήσκειν τολμᾶν), but they themselves no longer dared even to punish transgressors.[56] Plato's Socrates goes one stage further in the *Apology* (32a): to have any effect at all, anyone who really wants to fight for the right (τὸν τῷ ὄντι μαχούμενον ὑπὲρ τοῦ δικαίου), must renounce all ambition for political office. So in his own defence he will 'not yield to anyone through fear of death', just as earlier in a court of judgment he had been the only one to vote against an unjust judgment, despite the threats of the majority, because he believed that he 'must run the risk to the end with law and justice on my side', rather than follow the majority 'in an unjust judgment through fear of imprisonment or death' (32b/c). His refusal to escape from prison, despite the threat of execution, because of his respect for the laws of the city, sets the final seal on his attitude. For the ancient world, including Hellenistic Jews and Christians, he thus became the first example of the steadfast martyr for truth and justice.[57]

One further example worth mentioning is Hermias, the friend of Aristotle, who was crucified by the Great King. At the last, he sent from the cross a message to his friends that he had not done anything 'unworthy of philosophy or shameful'. Aristotle dedicated a paean to him, glorifying him along with Heracles, the Dioscuroi, Achilles and Ajax:

> O virtue, hard for the mortal race to attain,
> noblest prize that life can win,
> for the sake of your beauty, O virgin,
> death would be an enviable fate in Greece
> (σᾶς πέρι, παρθένε, μορφᾶς
> καὶ θανεῖν ζαλωτὸς ἐν ῾Ελλάδι πότμος)
> and to endure fierce untiring labours
> . . . for the sake of your fair form
> the nursling of Atarneus
> left the sunlit world.
> The Muses will make you immortal . . .

He too was a philosophical witness for truth against the cruelty of the tyrant.[58]

The Jewish freedom fighters in the time of the Maccabees could take up this philosophical tradition of fighting and dying for law, righteousness and divine truth, and use it to create a new type of martyr. However, a hitherto little noted verse in Ben Sira, who connects the new spirit of the age with the Old Testament tradition, shows that this idea had already entered Palestinian Judaism before the trial of fortitude under Antiochus IV Epiphanes: 'Fight to the death for righteousness and Yahweh will fight for you' (*'ad ham-māwet hēʿāṣeh 'al haṣ-ṣedeq wᵉyhwh nilḥām lākh*). His grandson translates: ἕως θανάτου ἀγώνισαι περὶ τῆς ἀληθείας, καὶ κύριος ὁ θεὸς πολεμήσει ὑπὲρ σοῦ.⁵⁹ Here we can already see something of the spirit which inspired, say, Mattathias and his sons a generation later. In II Macc. 13.14 Judas admonishes his followers before the battle 'to fight boldly to the death for (περί) law, sanctuary, city, fatherland and constitution', with the battle cry 'To God the victory' (θεοῦ νίκην, see p. 9 above). At this point the distinction between Palestinian and Hellenistic Judaism proves to be very relative and virtually meaningless. True, 'dying for the truth' appears much more rarely in ancient witnesses than dying 'for the *polis*' or for '*friends*', but – leaving aside Socrates – the fact that it is not completely absent even there is evident from the discussions which the hero of Philostratus' *Vita Apollonii* has with his two pupils Demetrius and Danis about the meaning of philosophical martyrdom before Apollonius voluntarily submits to Domitian's judgment in Rome. Demetrius advises him to escape, since a 'slave's death' is unworthy of philosophy. It befits the philosopher 'to die in the attempt either to liberate his city or to protect his parents, children, brothers or kinsfolk, or to die struggling for his friends, who to the wise man are more precious than mere kinsfolk.' Damis, the real successor of the teacher, is so impressed that he begins to question the readiness of the teacher to die. The execution would certainly be a triumph for the enemies of philosophy. So on the one hand Damis maintains the theory that 'one ought to die for philosophy' (ἀποθνήσκειν . . . ὑπὲρ φιλοσοφίας . . . δεῖν) in the sense of dying for one's temples and city walls, and the tombs of one's ancestors. For many famous men have gladly died to save such interests as these (ὑπὲρ σωτηρίας γὰρ τῶν τοιῶνδε). On the other hand, he does not regard such a death as meaningful now because of its disastrous consequences. Both are sharply contradicted by the hero: as a child of the East, dominated by fear, Damis does not know the nature of either true freedom or philosophy.

The wise man should indeed die for the things that have been mentioned, and of course any man would equally die for them without being wise, for it is an obligation of the law that we should die for freedom and an injunction of nature that we should die for kinsfolk or friends or loved ones. Now all men are the slaves of nature and law, the willing slaves of nature as the unwilling slaves of law. But it is the duty of the wise in a still higher degree to lay down their lives for tenets they have embraced (τελευτᾶν ὑπὲρ ὧν ἐπετήδευσαν). Here are interests which neither law has laid upon us nor nature planted in us from birth, but to which we have devoted ourselves out of mere strength of character and courage. On behalf of these, therefore, should anyone try to violate them, let the wise man pass through fire, let him bare his neck to the axe, for he will not be overcome by any such threats not driven to any sort of subterfuge, but he will maintain his conviction, as firmly as if it were a religion in which he had been initiated.

Since philosophical truth thus represents the ultimate religious obligation for Apollonius, he goes his way unhesitatingly at the risk of his life. In so doing, he does not betray his friends, 'but at the same time I will not betray myself either; but I will boldly wrestle with the tyrant, hailing him with the words of noble Homer, "Mars is as much my friend as yours".'[60]

According to Philostratus, Apollonius' attitude is essentially an illustration of the Cynics' criticism of all institutions: the conclusion shows how the heroic attitude of an Achilles or Hector is the model even for the philosophical ideal of the martyr. It seems to me that there is a knowledge of the gospel passion narratives and the attitude of the Jewish-Christian martyrs and a critical detachment from them. As a 'divine man', Apollonius knows in advance that the tyrant will not get the better of him, that he does not have to die. And indeed he is spirited away in a miraculous manner in the middle of the trial.

(v) Atoning sacrifice

In the early Greek period, the sacrifice of the individual for the good of the community was also often understood as an *expiatory sacrifice* to assuage the anger of the gods. Klaus Wengst,[61] who emphatically stressed the Greek origin of ἀποθνήσκειν ὑπέρ as a vicarious dying for others, wanted to ascribe the conception of cultic atonement only to the Old Testament and Jewish tradition, but he pays too little attention to the rich Greek material. Thus one could well claim that he seems to be inconsistent with his own views. Of course at the same time – as I have already stressed several times – here again we see the relativity of such traditio-historical 'attempts at derivation'. The theme of expiation in the sense of 'purifying the land' from evil and disaster or of 'assuaging' the wrath of the gods was part of the *lingua franca* of the religions of late antiquity. In this context it is particularly striking how many contacts can be demonstrated between ancient Greek ideas and those of the Old Testament. In the Graeco-Roman world in particular, the theme of expiation was often connected with a human sacrifice 'in the sense of an extraordinary atonement'.[62] Because there is a whole series of excellent studies on human sacrifice in the ancient world, representative atoning death and the conceptions and rites associated with it, e.g. the phenomenon of the '*pharmakos*',[63] I do not need to go into as much detail as in my discussion of 'dying for', and in what follows can keep to essentials. Of course at an early stage human sacrifice was already rejected as a barbaric custom, but despite this, in desperate circumstances it was used as a religious and political means in the time of Themistocles, and even under Caesar and Augustus.[64] Furthermore, certain forms of death penalty also had sacrificial features to them.[65] The same figures keep on being mentioned in ancient literature for their sacrifices: by his voluntary sacrifice, Menoeceus[66] atones for the ancient blood-guilt of Oedipus; the sacrifice of Iphigenia reconciles angry Artemis and opens up the way for the sack of Troy;[67] the sacrifice of Polyxena appeases the spirit of Achilles and thus guarantees the safety of the victors' return;[68] King Erechtheus is to still the wrath of Poseidon by the sacrifice of a daughter, but instead of one daughter, all three of his daughters go to their deaths.[69]

Greek tragedy above all saw that the theme of the atoning death of individual prominent figures of mythical antiquity remained alive among all strata of the population. For Aeschylus, the sacrifice of Iphigenia takes on decisive significance as the reason for the disaster which comes upon Agamemnon and his family. Sophocles wrote dramas about both Polyxena and Iphigenia.

Above all, however, it was the plays of Euripides at the beginning of the Greek enlightenment[70] which in a striking way took up the theme of an atoning or sacrificial death and explained it in terms of 'voluntary sacrifice of one's life for a higher end'. In six of the extant tragedies (*Alcestis, Heraclides, Hecuba, Supplices, Phoenissae*), and in at least three of the lost ones (*Protesilaus, Erechtheus* and *Phrixos*), this plays a prominent role.[71]

With the exception of the *Alcestis*, where the 'vicarious death' (ὑπεραποθνήσκειν), like the 'imitative death' (ἐπαποθνήσκειν) of Evadne in the *Supplices* and of Laodameia in the *Protesilaus*, is in each case for love, an atoning death always has explicit cultic features. It is striking here that 'in his accounts of sacrificial deaths, even those which are his own invention, the poet has closely followed the Greek sacrificial ritual in every detail'. This is a σφάγιον, i.e. a blood sacrifice, of the kind which is offered to the powers of the underworld before great undertakings, battle, taking an oath or sacrificing to the dead. 'As human sacrifices, of course they have far greater value and greater effectiveness . . . and are in and for themselves guarantees of victory.'[72] An essential feature of this rite was the shedding of blood by cutting the throat in ritual fashion; this provided an association with the underworld which in Euripides is embodied especially by Persephone. It is remarkable how this 'enlightened' tragedian combines an ethical rejection of human sacrifice with a realistic account of this cruel archaic rite. The decisive reason for his doing this was to portray the hero or heroine's voluntary sacrifice of life, by which he gave a last degree of intensification to the conflict of tragedy. Another factor may be that at the same time there was some contribution from the glorification of the sacrificial death for all Greece or for a threatened native city, which was so popular in the political crises of the fifth century.[73] Nevertheless, an element remains which is difficult to elucidate, the knowledge that the primal dark and oppressive experience of the connection between guilt and fate and the need for expiation cannot simply be removed by the reasoning of an enlightenment. Roussel comments:[74]

nous apercevons le sentiment antique de l'efficacité du sacrifice pour la conservation de la vie sociale. Euripide est pénétré de ce sentiment, et l'a traduit magnifiquement dans son oeuvre . . . Dans tous les périodes de grandes crises, l'utilité pratique du dévouement total de l'individu à la communauté ne se traduit-il pas par le sentiment mystique de la valeur expiatoire et pro-pitiatoire du sang librement répandu?

Indeed, we also owe to Euripides the most irrational, ecstatic and cruel of all the ancient dramas, the *Bacchae*, in which the fearful end of Pentheus essentially also represents a sacrifice. Above all through his plays, which were so frequently performed, the idea of the heroic, voluntary and vicarious sacrificial death for the good of the homeland became familiar to the whole Graeco-Roman world.

Of course the subject appears in ancient sagas very much more frequently than in the mythical material used by Euripides. In the seventh century, i.e. already in the historical period, the 'crime of Cylon', a political murder in a holy place, as a result of which plague broke out in Athens, is said to have been expiated by the voluntary sacrifice of two young men.[75] This theme was especially popular in connection with the self-sacrifice of sisters, who in deep need save their threatened homeland through their common sacrificial death.[76] W. Burkert would describe this sacrifice of virgins, which is particularly prominent in Euripides also, from primal hunting and fighting societies, who used this rite to prepare themselves for going out to battle.[77] At all events, the archaic character of this motive is obvious.

Some examples are impressive to the New Testament scholar simply because of the cultic language they use. Thus the two daughters of Orion in Aeonia in Boeotia declare themselves ready in time of plague to propitiate the two gods of the underworld (ἱλάσσασθαι τοὺς δύο ἐριουνίους θεούς) by 'accepting death for their fellow citizens' (ὑπὲρ ἀστῶν θάνατον ἐδέξαντο). Of their own free will they offered themselves to the gods as sacrifices (αὐτοῖς ἑκοῦσαι θύματα γίνονται). However, Hades and Persephone had mercy on them and transported them as stars to the heavens. Their fellow citizens built a temple to them, 'with annual celebrations and sacrifices for the propitiation of the dead'.[78] The tourist Pausanias was able to visit the pyre and ashes of two other Boeotian sisters who are said to have sacrificed themselves willingly in place of their father in order to save their native city of Thebes.[79] In Athens, the daughters of the primal king Erechtheus (see n. 69 above) were not the only ones to kill themselves to assuage the wrath of Poseidon. According to a kindred saga, the three daughters of Leo, the Leokorai, were sacrificed during a plague or a famine. People also built a sanctuary in their honour, the Leokorion.[80] There is a similar account of the four daughters of Hyacinthus, an immigrant from Lacedaimonia to Athens.[81] Aglauros, one of the daughters of Cecrops and a priestess of Athens, is said to have hurled herself from the walls to save the city as a result of an oracle of Apollo when war threatened. She also had a sanctuary, in which the ephebes of Attica swore their oath.[82] The theme of the purity of those consecrated always played a decisive role in these virgin sacrifices. The theme itself remains almost the same, though names and individual features from these sagas could easily be exchanged, confused and varied. This shows the importance of the actual theme.

Men, too, offered themselves as sacrifices in a similar way. Reference has already been made to king Codrus of Athens. When the Dioscuroi invaded Attica, a foreigner by the name of Marathon is said to have sacrificed himself willingly before the battle;[83] the city received its name from him. The saga is possibly an invention from the Persian period, in the same way as Euripides 'invented' the sacrifice of Macaria, the daughter of Heracles.[84]

Finally, one could also refer to the representative death of one individual for another. Quite apart from the death of Alcestis for her husband Admetus (see p. 9 above), the theme appears in the case of the wise centaur Cheiron, who, wounded by Heracles' poisoned arrow, made over his immortality to Prometheus in order to avoid eternal putrefaction. We find the same thing in the imperial period in the form of a promise to make over one's own life for the emperor, as in the case of Augustus, Caligula, Otho or Hadrian.[85]

This list of examples could be continued, but I must break it off at this point. One fixed ingredient of almost all these traditions is that the voluntary sacrifice did not rest on a man's own decision, but followed the divine demand of an atoning sacrifice to deliver the people, the land or a family, which was given by a seer or an oracle, often that of Delphi.[86]

Conceptions universal in antiquity, widespread and going back to the earliest period, underlie these sagas of atoning sacrifices which seem to us to be so cruel.[87] Historical and psychological explanations of them can no longer bring us complete satisfaction. The depth of the crisis brought about by guilt and destiny is matched by the magnitude of the demand for unconditional sacrifice. At the deepest level, doom and sin were related. The voluntary nature of such sacrifice, stressed from the time of Euripides on, gave it ultimate moral stature and made it a model for citizens.

The Roman *devotio* of a general in desperate situations in war, already mentioned above, can also be fitted into the framework of such sacrifice. It is often described directly as an expiatory sacrifice (*piaculum*). According to Livy, the general P. Decius hurled himself on his foes 'like a messenger from heaven to expiate all anger of the gods and to turn aside destruction from his people and bring it on their adversaries'. All this after he had dedicated himself as a *devotus* on the basis of a dream.[88] His son also dedicated himself as a *devotus*, appealing to the example of his father: 'It is the privilege of our family that we should be sacrificed to avert the nation's perils. Now I will offer up the legions of the enemy, to be slain with myself as victims to Earth and the gods of the underworld.'[89] In his *Pharsalia*, Lucan depicts the death of the younger Cato as *devotio*, which atones for the blood-guilt of the civil war. The climax of the remarks addressed to Brutus, a remarkable mixture of Stoic philosophy, Roman religion and visions of apocalyptic horror, consists in the following praise: 'So

may it be: may the strict gods of the Romans receive complete
expiation, and may we not cheat war of any of its victims. If only
the gods of heaven and the underworld would allow this head to
expose itself to all punishment as one condemned! The hordes of
the enemy cast down Decius, the consecrated one: may the two
armies (involved in the civil war) pierce me through. May the
barbarians from the Rhine make me the target of their shots, and
exposed to every spear, may I receive all the wounds of the whole
war. This my blood will ransom all the people; this my death will
achieve atonement for all that the Romans have deserved through
their moral decline.'⁹⁰ The writer of these words, M. Annaeus
Lucan, was a contemporary of Paul's, and nephew of Seneca. He
died on 30 April, AD 65, at the age of twenty-five, on Nero's orders.
These words help us to understand why the earliest Christian
message made sense in Rome.

If we look for a summary characterization of these expiatory
rites and those involved in them, we come up against the term
pharmakos, the specifically Greek form of the 'scapegoat'. We find
it in archaic times in a number of cities, especially in Ionia, and
including Athens. There year by year a particular man was driven
out of the city or even killed in accordance with a fixed rite of
humiliation to secure the purification of the country.⁹¹ The best-
known example of this custom is the driving out or stoning of two
people during the feast of Thargelia in Athens, which was dedicated to Apollo: 'one for the men and one for the women' (ἕνα
μὲν ὑπὲρ τῶν ἀνδρῶν, ἕνα δὲ ὑπὲρ τῶν γυναικῶν). Istrus, a pupil
of Callimachus, who lived in the third century BC, derived it from
a certain Pharmakos who had stolen the sacred vessels belonging to
Apollo: he had been caught by the people of Achilles and stoned.
This is a preposterous and artificial aetiology, which goes back to
one of the Ionian cities, possibly Miletus.⁹² We need not trouble
ourselves further with the question of the original form and
derivation of these ancient rites, over which scholars have been so
much in dispute; the important thing to note is its elaboration and
interpretation in the late Hellenistic and Roman period.

The most striking thing about the accounts is that as a rule they
are concerned with men who are poor, incapable of work, crippled

and maimed, who of necessity have 'sold' themselves for the common good; elsewhere, we have condemned criminals. This is in complete contrast to the heroic sagas according to which kings – like Codrus in the garments of a slave – princes or beautiful maidens offered themselves voluntarily for the common good. The scholia on Aristophanes and Aeschylus state in different ways that 'quite worthless and useless people' were 'sacrificed' as *pharmakoi*.[93] They were killed after being taken round the city, outside the gates, either through stoning or through being hurled from a rock. Their being led round the city was usually coupled with a curse.[94] At a later stage people were usually content with driving them beyond the bounds of the city by throwing stones at them. Thus their killing could be described as θύειν or as θυσία. A similar 'sacrifice' was offered on Rhodes to Kronos (ἐθύετο ἄνθρωπος τῷ Κρόνῳ), or they kept a criminal condemned to death until the festival of Kronos and then led him outside the gates (ἔξω πυλῶν) and killed him 'in front of the temple of Artemis Aristobule' (Porphyry, *De abstinentia* 2,54, Nauck p. 279). Heb. 13.12f. might remind its ancient audience of similar analogies.

On the island of Leucas, every year in a sacrifice for Apollo (ἐν τῇ θυσίᾳ τοῦ 'Απόλλωνος) a criminal was thrown into the sea from a rock to 'ward off evil' (ἀποτροπῆς χάριν). Later, people attempted to fish the unfortunate man out of the sea and bring him to dry land. In this way the original human sacrifice was commuted.[95] Ovid (*Ibis*, 467f.) reports that the citizens of Abdera killed the one 'devoted to death' with a hail of stones. For him the ancient Ionian rite is simply a special form of *devotio*:

Aut te devoveat certis Abdera diebus
Saxaque devotum grandine plura petant.
(Or the city of Abdera could devote you to death on
particular days, and catch the one devoted under a hail
of stones.)[96]

The scholia interpreted these obscure sentences in rather different ways. According to an earlier tradition, going back to Callimachus (third century BC), year by year the whole city was purified (*uno quoque anno totam civatatem publice lustrabant*) when the people of Abdera stoned one of its citizens whom they had 'devoted' for this day, 'for the salvation of each individual citizen' (*pro capitibus omnium*). Another scholiast says that in Abdera 'a man was *sacrificed for the sins of the citizens*, but people proscribed him seven days earlier, so that in this way he alone would take upon himself the sins of all' (*hominem inmolari pro peccatis civium ut sic omnium peccata solus haberet*). There is clear evidence of the influence of Christian terminology on this last text (cf. I Cor. 15.3; Gal. 1.4: *pro peccatis nostris*; Isa. 53.12: *et ipse peccatum multorum tulit*). In the Diegesis on fragment 90 of the *Aitiae* of Callimachus, which has been preserved on papyrus, of course we only hear that the Abderites bought a man, whom they then fed for a period, and then took him round the city outside the walls as a 'means of purification for the city' (καθάρσιον τῆς πόλεως), finally driving him outside the territory of the city by throwing stones at him.[97] Here the tradition has evidently accentuated the real custom. There also seems to me evidence of the influence of Christian tradition in the poem of the Byzantine writer Tzetzes (twelfth century AD) about the *pharmakos*, which could go back to verses of the poet Hipponax (sixth century BC), who reports of the customs of Ionian cities: 'they took the most hateful of all as to a sacrifice' (cf. Isa. 53.3), τῶν πάντων ἀμορφότερον ἦγον ὡς πρὸς θυσίαν, 'they made the sacrifice at the appropriate place', εἰς τόπον δὲ τὸν πρόσφορον στήσαντες τὴν θυσίαν. The corpse of the *pharmakos* was burnt with the wood of wild trees and his ashes were scattered on the sea.[98]

This theme appears even in a Christian martyr legend in the fifth or sixth century AD, the Martyrdom of Caesarius,[99] which is quite unhistorical and has novellistic features, set in Terracina, between Rome and Naples. There frivolous young men are said to have been convinced that they should live a riotous life for a period at the expense of the community and then on an appointed day be hurled from a rock in full war attire 'for the salvation of the state, the emperor, and the wellbeing of the citizens' (*pro salute rei publicae et principum et civium salubritate*), not to mention their own glory (*et ut nomen habeat gloriae*). The corpses of the victims were brought to the temple of Apollo with great veneration and there burnt; the ashes were kept *pro salute rei publicae et civium*. The saint protested against this barbaric custom and thus caused his imprisonment. The narrative shows how in a later period the ancient rite was elaborated by the inclusion of traditional elements, while at the same time the pagan custom was transformed into an antitype of the Christian veneration of martyrs. It is significant that the traditional killing (or expulsion) of a poor or sick man to purify the city was transformed into an honourable event for the salvation of all.

A very ancient form of purifying a city from plague by stoning a *pharmakos* probably underlies the saga, related by Philostratus, of the overcoming of the plague in Ephesus by Apollonius of Tyana. He had the whole population of the city assembled in the theatre before the statue of Heracles Apotropaeus; in the crowd he saw a poor and apparently blind beggar whom he made the crowd bury under a mountain of stones (in fact he embodied the plague demon). When the stones were taken away, the people found under the corpse of a giant dog (*Vita Apollonii* 4.10). In order to liberate or purify the city, the *pharmakos*, as the incarnation of the disaster which brought the corruption, had to vanish – i.e. either be covered with stones or be plagued in the sea or – as a humane mitigation – be driven out. The Byzantine *Lexica* still report from unknown sources that the *pharmakos* was cast into the sea as a sacrifice for Poseidon with the cry, 'Be our means of atonement, that is, salvation and redemption' (περίψημα ἡμῶν γενοῦ, ἤτοι σωτηρία καὶ ἀπολύτρωσις).)'[100]

When Paul describes himself and other apostles of Jesus Christ as περίψημα and περικαθάρματα τοῦ κόσμου he is taking up this old conception. Both terms had become vicious taunts (I Cor. 4.13). The most impressive description of the '*pharmakos*' in Greek drama is to be found in the figure of Sophocles' Oedipus,[101] who, to atone for the evil which he has unwittingly committed and to rid the land of a murderous curse, blinds himself and allows himself to be driven from home. As a criminal doomed to destruction (ἀσεβής, 1441), he wanders from place to place, homeless and in poverty, until he finds reconciliation, a home and a solution at the sacred shrine of the Eumenides in Colonus in Attica. For in the end death has lost all terrors for him; it is a mysterious transformation:

> For no mortal could say what death he died,
> but only Theseus.
> No gleaming flash of divine fire took him away,
> nor a whirlwind from the sea – but he was taken.
> It was a messenger from heaven,
> or else some gentle, painless opening of the earth.
> For without a sigh, or disease, or pain,
> he passed away – an end most marvellous,
> like no other man.[102]

Thus his end is divine grace

> For where as a grace (χάρις)
> the night is preserved below,
> there is no mourning.[103]

Oedipus, whose peaceful passage over the threshold of death is in the end veiled in divine mystery, at the same time achieves atonement through his measureless suffering. Thus his figure as portrayed in Sophocles' two plays may now show the most kindred features in all Greek drama – for all the fundamental differences – to the story of the passion and resurrection of Jesus in the gospels. Oedipus, too, knows that one who is well-meaning can intercede for many and expiate the Eumenides. At the request of the elders to propitiate the goddesses of the holy place, he sends Antigone:

> For I believe that one soul can intercede
> for thousands, to expiate this – it approaches in good pleasure
> ἀρκεῖν γὰρ οἶμαι κἀντὶ μυρίων μίαν
> ψυχὴν τάδ' ἐκτίνουσαν, ἢν εὔνους παρῇ (498f.)

(vi) The atoning death of Christ and the Graeco-Roman world

Thus we have answered more than adequately the question with which we began, whether the pagan audiences in Antioch, Ephesus, Corinth and Rome could have understood the new message of the atoning death of Jesus and the conceptions of vicariousness, atonement and reconciliation associated with it. The Gentile who heard the gospel was quite familiar in his own way not only with the hero's self-chosen death as a way to apotheosis *per aspera ad astra* and the theme of vicarious dying for others out of love, but also with the notion of a voluntary death as an atoning sacrifice, and he could also understand it in his own way. True, customs of this kind might seem archaic or barbaric to him, but he knew them through myth, patriotic sagas and dramas, and they were at the same time transfigured by the heroic and mythical framework.

The ambivalence of the ancient audience towards narratives of this kind is evident from an account by Plutarch, who was similarly a contemporary of the New Testament writers (*c.* AD 45–120). He tells how the Leuctrides Korai, once violated by the Spartans, appeared to Pelopidas in a dream before the battle of Leuctra. The daughters of Skedasos, they had committed suicide out of shame at their disgrace, and their father had followed suit. Their tombs were in the plain of Leuctra. 'Ever after, prophecies and oracles kept warning the Spartans to be on watchful guard against the Leuctrian wrath' (μηνίμα, cf. Pausanias 9.13.5). The maidens commanded the general to sacrifice a virgin with auburn hair if he wished to win the victory over his enemies. 'The injunction seemed a dreadful and lawless (παράνομος) one to him', but he took the advice of seers and other officers:

> Some of these would not hear of the injunction being neglected or disobeyed, adducing as examples of such sacrifice among the ancients, Menoeceus, son of Creon, Macaria, daughter of Heracles; and in later times, Pherecydes the wise man, who was put to death by the Lacedaemonians, and whose skin was preserved by their kings, in accordance with some oracle; and Leonidas, who, in obedience to the oracle, sacrificed himself, as it were, to save Greece; and still further, the youths who were sacrificed by Themistocles to Dionysus Carnivorous before the sea fight at Salamis; for the successes which followed these sacrifices proved them acceptable to the gods. Moreover, when Agesilaus, who was setting out on an expedition from the same place as Agamemnon did, and against the same enemies, was asked by the goddess for his daughter in sacrifice, and had this vision as he lay asleep at Aulis, he was too tender-hearted to give

her, and thereby brought his expedition to an unsuccessful and inglorious ending. Others, on the contrary, argued against it, declaring that such a barbarous and lawless (παράνομος) sacrifice was not acceptable to any one of the superior beings above us, for it was not the fabled typhons and giants who governed the world, but the father of all gods and men; even to believe in the existence of divine beings who take delight in the slaughter and blood of men was perhaps a folly (ἀβέλτερον), but if such beings existed, they must be disregarded, as having no power; for only weakness and depravity of soul could produce or harbour such unnatural and cruel desires.

(22) While, then, the chief men were thus disputing, and while Pelopidas in particular was in perplexity, a filly broke away from the herd of horses and sped through the camp, and when she came to the very place of their conference, stood still. The rest only admired the colour of her glossy mane, which was fiery red, her high mettle, and the vehemence and boldness of her neighing; but Theocritus the seer, after taking thought, cried out to Pelopidas: 'Your sacrificial victim is come, good man; so let us not wait for any other virgin; accept and use the one which heaven offers you.' So they took the mare and led her to the tombs of the maidens upon which, after decking her with garlands and consecrating her with prayers, they sacrificed her.[104]

Only Plutarch tells the story in this form. Earlier historians like Xenophon, and also Diodore, merely report that the sacrifice took place near the tombs; according to Xenophon the Thebans had decorated them, since they had been encouraged by an oracle that they would win there. The romance-like elaboration in Plutarch shows his own theory of religion. On the one hand there is still a belief in the efficacy of archaic rites, especially as people revered the heroes of ancient times who had sacrificed themselves. However, such primal religious sense could not be reconciled with the purified understanding of religion to be found in the enlightenment. Human sacrifices were regarded as 'barbaric' and 'criminal', and the Romans had therefore rightly prohibited them among the

Druids and the Carthaginians. They were not required by any divine being, least of all by the supreme god, Zeus. If any kind of demons, i.e. probably the souls of criminals, '*biothanati*', wanted human blood, they had to be refused it categorically. The division between ancient religious experience and enlightened ethical thought is resolved, *providentia dei*, in the happiest of ways. The seer recognizes that the dream is fulfilled in the filly which comes trotting along. The battle thus leads to the defeat of the Spartans and the end of their predominance in Greece.

The message of the death of Jesus of Nazareth, the Son of God, on the cross for all men was not incomprehensible even to the educated audience of the Gentile world. Its linguistic and religious categories were largely familiar to this audience. Nevertheless, the primitive Christian preaching of the crucified Messiah must have seemed aesthetically and ethically repulsive to them and to be in conflict with the philosophically purified nature of the gods. The new doctrine of salvation had not only barbarian, but also irrational and excessive features. It appeared to contemporaries as a dark or even mad superstition.[105] For this was not the death of a hero from ancient times, suffused in the glow of religion, but that of a Jewish craftsman of the most recent past, executed as a criminal, with whom the whole present and future salvation of all men was linked. Because of this, the earliest Christian mission always spoke also of the teaching, the actions and the passion of the Messiah from Galilee. The narrative about his messianic person was part of the preaching of the cross.

On the other hand, the Christian message fundamentally broke apart the customary conceptions of atonement in the ancient world and did so at many points. For example, it spoke not of atonement for a particular crime, but of universal atonement for *all* human guilt. Furthermore, it was decisive that God's grace was given, not as the result of the heroic action of a particular man, but by God himself, through Jesus, the Son, who was delivered over to death (II Cor. 5.18ff.). In other words, men no longer need to assuage the wrath of God through their actions. God, as subject of the saving event, reconciled to himself his unfaithful creatures, who had become his enemies. Finally, the Christian message took on its ultimate acuteness and urgency as a result of its *eschatological* character. The atoning death of the Son of God and reconciliation came about in the face of the imminent judgment of the world. All this was said in language and conceptuality which was not essentially strange to the men of the Greek and Roman world.

When fundamental difficulties in understanding arise, they are felt not by the audience of ancient times, Jewish or Gentile, but by us, the men of today. However, precisely because of this difficulty in understanding today, we must guard against limiting, for apologetic reasons, the fundamental significance of the soteriological interpretation of the death of Jesus as vicarious atonement in the context of the earliest Christian preaching. Today we find not only a 'fundamentalist' but also a radical critical biblicism, which seeks to strip Jesus and the earliest Christian message, as far as possible, of all that it regards as 'mythological' and therefore as theologically obsolete. Over against this, as scientific exegetes, we must attempt to illustrate, first of all, the origin of this central expression of the faith of the earliest church with all the philological and historical means at our disposal, so that we can understand it in terms of its earliest presuppositions.

II

The Origin of the Soteriological Interpretation of the Death of Jesus

An attempt to answer the questions raised at the end of the previous chapter should also help us to answer three further basic questions which arise out of what has been said so far:

(*a*) What was the specific feature of the primitive Christian expression of the vicarious atoning death of Jesus which distinguished it from analogous Greek and Jewish conceptions? Why was this message evidently offensive and at the same time victorious, and what made it new?

(*b*) To what degree is there a connection between the soteriological interpretation of the death of Jesus and the Old Testament and Jewish tradition, especially as right at the very start primitive Christianity was a Jewish Palestinian movement of an apocalyptic and messianic character?

(*c*) At the same time this raises the question of the age and the origins of this tradition. Does it enter the early primitive Christian kerygma at a relatively late stage as a secondary 'interpretative element', perhaps only in the so-called Hellenistic Jewish-Christian community, or from the beginning was it a constitutive element of the Christian message?

One might also ask: did it only so to speak come in by means of later theological reflection by the 'Hellenistic community' or is it inseparably bound up with the Easter event itself? Indeed, in essence does it perhaps go back to the words and actions of Jesus himself?

An answer to the third question will also provide answers to the first and second.

(i) *Pauline formulae and pre-Pauline tradition*

The best and most sensible method is to turn to the earliest texts, the authentic letters of Paul, which were written only twenty to twenty-five years after the event which founded the earliest community. They·bring us closest in time and content to the earliest preaching of the primitive community to which we have access.

By contrast, the account of the earliest period of the community in Acts is about thirty years later, and despite the use of 'archaic' material in the speeches of Peter, which are significant for our questions, the hand of the redactor is very evident. In contrast to the account given by Luke of what is supposed to be the earliest primitive Christian kerygma in the speeches in Acts, with the best will in the world one cannot claim that statements about the vicarious death of Jesus 'for us' play only a minor role in the letters of Paul. Formulae and statements which express the saving significance of the death of Jesus are too frequent and too varied in the writing of the greatest missionary and theologian of primitive Christianity to be ignored, and the stereotyped form of some of them already points back to earlier traditions.

The fact that soteriological formulae of this kind retreat right into the background in the synoptic tradition is quite another matter. Nevertheless, even there we find explicit formulae at two highly significant points: Mark 10.45 (= Matt. 20.28) and then in the tradition of the Last Supper (Mark 14.24 = Matt. 26.28). The fact that they are otherwise lacking is no indication that they were unknown to the authors of the synoptic gospels. The reason for their lack of prominence is rather that understandably they do not play a central role in the proclamation of Jesus. In the first place he sought to announce the dawn of the kingdom of God, and in the face of this task his own fate retreated into the background. It is even possible that Luke's unique restraint over against a soteriological interpretation of the death of Jesus may be explained by the fact that this first historian of early Christianity is oriented on the Jesus tradition, which is exemplary as far as he is concerned.

By contrast the allegedly independent, decidedly post-Easter 'theologies' of the so-called Q or Marcan 'communities', detached completely from the person of Jesus, are artificial products of modern exegesis. We may not refer to them in any way to claim that in earliest Christianity there was also a kerygma in which the death and resurrection of Jesus played no part, or only a small part. Q and Mark did not set out to present 'community theology', but primarily the message and the work of Jesus. Where in Mark the influence of the theology of the evangelist becomes visible, the death of Jesus becomes important too (below pp. 42ff.).

In Paul we find stereotyped expressions about the atoning death of Jesus chiefly in two forms: first, in statements which express the *'giving up'* of Jesus for our salvation, connected with the composite verb παραδιδόναι or the simple διδόναι. This so-called 'surrender formula' is, of course, very variable, so it is taking a liberty to describe it as a fixed formula.[1] In two cases God himself is the one who 'gives up'. One is in Rom. 8.32, where he appears as subject: 'He who did not spare his own Son but gave him up for us all.' Here the first line has a reference to Gen. 22.12, the sacrifice of Isaac (καὶ οὐκ ἐφείσω τοῦ υἱοῦ σου τοῦ ἀγαπητοῦ δι'ἐμέ).

On the other hand, in the two-membered formula of Rom. 4.25 we find a divine passive:

Who was given up (ὃς παρεδόθη) for (διά) our trespasses and raised for (διά) our justification.

It is very probable that this statement depends on Isa. 53.12. In Gal. 1.4; 2.20 and the Deutero-Pauline texts Eph. 5.2, 25; Titus 2.14 and I Tim. 2.6, Christ is the subject who gave up his life himself 'for us'. In the last instance this surrender of his life is described as a 'ransom' (ἀντίλυτρον); thus the verse proves to be a variant of the earlier Semitic-type expression, Mark 10.45, in the Greek tradition.

In all the Pauline and Deutero-Pauline texts the preposition is *hyper*, with the exception of Rom. 4.25, where the *dia* goes back to the influence of Isa. 53.12 LXX, and Gal. 1.14, where the textual variant *peri* is possibly original. Of course there is much dispute as to the origin of this 'surrender formula'. If we look for an Old Testament model, we quickly come upon Isa. 53, where in the LXX the verb *paradidonai* appears three times for the surrendering of the servant of God and is twice related to 'our sins' (53.6, 12).

This is in accordance with the traditional interpretation,[2] which, however, is now under considerable attack. As Werner Grimm has shown very recently,[3] we should also add Isa. 43.3f., as this text has relatively close connections with the earliest form of our tradition, Mark 10.45.[4] Of course, this does not yet have any decisive bearing on the 'antiquity' of this tradition. We shall therefore begin by leaving aside this whole complex and turn to other more important and more fixed groups of formulae in Paul, as they help us more to make a proper historical move back to the obscure 'pre-Pauline' period of the formation of early Christian formulae.

The second, so-called 'dying formula',[5] is primarily limited to Paul himself. Its best known expression is to be found in the summary of Paul's gospel with a catechetical form to be found in I Cor. 15.3b: Χριστὸς ἀπέθανεν ὑπὲρ τῶν ἁμαρτιῶν ἡμῶν. Otherwise, however, Paul usually uses this formula in an abbreviated form: Χριστὸς ἀπέθανεν ὑπὲρ ἡμῶν (or something similar). Here the shorter form only becomes fully comprehensible in the light of the longer form: ὑπὲρ ἡμῶν means 'for the forgiveness of our sins', by which we have separated ourselves from God. This is the case even in the pre-Pauline and extra-Pauline tradition, as Paul uses the plural 'sins' and the conception of forgiveness only very rarely. Isaiah 53 may have some influence on the longer form. This could be indicated not only by the striking ὑπὲρ τῶν ἁμαρτιῶν (cf. Gal. 1.4) but also by the κατὰ τὰς γραφάς, which is unique for Paul. The constitutive elements of both the longer and shorter formulae are the subject Χριστός; the aorist ἀπέθανεν, which refers to a unique, unrepeatable event of the past (cf. Rom. 6.9f.); and the preposition ὑπέρ with the genitive, which contains the soteriological interpretation. Of course this formula too is variable, and its particular form depends on the context. The subject Χριστός in the formula appears seven times (I Cor. 15.3; Rom. 5.6, 8; 14.9; I Cor. 8.11; Gal. 2.21; I Peter 3.18; cf. also I Thess. 5.10); the verb ἀποθνῄσκειν in the aorist on the other hand appears ten times (I Cor. 15.3b; Rom. 5.6, 8; Rom. 14.9; I Cor. 8.11; II Cor. 5.14, 15 twice; Gal. 2.21; I Thess. 5.10 aorist participle; I Peter 3.18 as a *varia lectio* of ἔπαθεν).[6] Paul uses the preposition ὑπέρ even more often in the soteriological sense, and in addition it also dominates the surrender formulae. I Cor. 1.13; II Cor. 5.21; Gal. 3.13; indeed even Rom. 6.2, 8–10 seem to me to be dependent on the dying formula.

For Paul, the long form of I Cor. 15.3b is part of a 'paradosis' which he handed on to the Corinthians, on the founding of the community in AD 49/50, as a 'key element' (ἐν πρώτοις) and summary of his gospel. For him this is a matter of objective events taking place in time and space which at the same time possess ultimate, unsurpassable, in short, 'eschatological' saving significance.

In I Cor. 15.3–5 (or –8), in essentials we have a highly compressed historical account presented in credal form, which of course is inseparably fused with theological interpretative elements. These include above all the ὑπέρ τῶν ἁμαρτιῶν ἡμῶν but also the subject Χριστός, which in this confessional text has its original significance as a title and points to the death of the Messiah. For Greeks, Χριστός was completely unusual as a name, this is still evident from the way in which in Suetonius (and probably also in Tacitus)[7] it is confused with the slaves' name Χριστός; however, Christians in Antioch and in the Pauline communities were of course very well aware of the derivation of this unique name from the biblical eschatological expectation.

Along with the resurrection formula θεὸς ἤγειρεν τὸν Ἰησοῦν ἐκ νεκρῶν, the short formula Χριστὸς ἀπέθανεν ὑπὲρ ἡμῶν is the most frequent and most important confessional statement in the Pauline epistles and at the same time in the primitive Christian tradition in the Greek language which underlies them. The significance of I Cor. 15.3f. lies in the fact that here two formulae were linked together in an expanded form, whereas the other relatively infrequent two-membered formulae in Paul which link statements about dying and rising again are mostly abbreviated. I Corinthians 15.3 is therefore nearest in content to the two-membered formula Rom. 4.25, which has an independent tradition

from it. Thus if we are concerned with the age of the paradosis I Cor.
15.3f., the starting point is clear.[8] Paul passed it on in fixed form
to the young Christians in Corinth on the founding of their
community, and he retains it unaltered five or six years later when
he writes I Corinthians. The christological basis of the Pauline
kerygma has a firm shape and did not undergo any essential
metamorphoses. Evidently the tradition of I Cor. 15.3 had been
subjected to many tests in the long missionary activity of the apostle.
In content it points back through the people it lists (leaving aside
Paul himself) to Palestine and above all to Jerusalem. Thus this
piece of tradition explains why, despite all difficulties, the apostle
tries to hang on so persistently, to some degree almost at any price,
to the link he has with the centre of Judaism. One might assume
that it had already had fundamental significance in Paul's fourteen-
year-long missionary work in Syria and Cilicia, indeed that it had
even provided the common starting-point for the meeting between
Paul and Barnabas and the pillars in Jerusalem (Gal. 2.1–10),
from which agreement might be sought.[9] In terms of content it was
the foundation of that 'gospel' which Paul proclaimed to the
Gentiles and which he 'put before' the Jerusalem authorities
(Gal. 2.2). The closing sentence in I Cor. 15.11 gives a specific
indication of this: 'Whether then it was I or they, so we preach and
so you believed.' The ἐκεῖνοι who preach the same thing as Paul
are the preachers of the gospel from Peter on who are listed here.
At the same time, we should not forget that when he founded the
community in Corinth, Paul was accompanied by a missionary
partner from Jerusalem, Silas-Silvanus (I Thess. 1.1; Acts 15.40).
Thus one could say that the form of the paradosis goes back to the
early period of Paul's activity in Antioch and Syria, and indeed
even back as far as Damascus, but that its content in nearly all its
statements refers back to Jerusalem. The much disputed question
whether there was an original Aramaic form loses its significance in
the light of this. For the Greek-speaking Jewish-Christian community had its roots in Jerusalem itself. Jerusalem was a multi-
lingual city with a large Greek-speaking minority. In essentials,
we may assume that from the time of the formation of the community of Jerusalem by the event of Pentecost there was also a

Greek-speaking group there, which then soon became independent and translated the new message and the still living Jesus tradition into Greek.[10]

The long and hotly disputed contrast between 'Hellenistic' and 'Palestinian-Jewish' origins thus becomes a matter of only relative importance – at least as far as 'Hellenistic' origins are concerned. Of course we can hardly assume that Jewish, Aramaic or Hebrew texts came into being in the Diaspora of the Roman Empire outside Palestine – even in Phoenicia and Syria people spoke Greek in the synagogues, and Mesopotamia was part of the Parthian empire – but Greek texts could very well have been written also in Jewish Palestine, in Jerusalem as well as in Tiberias or Sepphoris. 'Hellenistic' and 'Palestinian-Jewish' need therefore no longer be in direct opposition. In any case, we can only talk about the Aramaic-speaking community in Palestine in a very limited and indirect way, because its own tradition has largely been lost. This cannot in any way be identified simply with Q and other parts of the synoptic tradition. In effect we know much more about Jesus than about the community around James; in addition, it is striking that James, the brother of Jesus, who later became leader of the Christian community, plays no part whatsoever in the synoptic tradition. The only mention of him, Mark 6.3 (= Matt. 13.55), has no positive significance whatsoever. This must really tell in favour of its originality.

(ii) *The crucified Messiah*

Of course, general considerations of this kind only help us to determine very roughly the age of the paradosis; it *may* come from the circle of the Hellenists in Jerusalem, but that is not necessarily the case. In order to fix it more precisely, we need to make a more thorough analysis of its individual elements. Here the subject and predicate Χριστὸς ἀπέθανεν, i.e. 'the Messiah died', are of prime interest.

We know that as a result of the Gentile mission in Antioch round about the middle of the thirties, the messianic title *Christos* gradually became a proper name, and Christians finally came to be called

Χριστιανοί, as a sect bound up with a person. Accordingly, the acclamation Χριστός ᾽Ιησοῦς became a double name. Of course this process must have taken years, and the messianic, titular meaning of Christ continued to be present in the church at a later stage as well. Like the formula 'God has raised (the man) Jesus from the dead', the phrase 'the Messiah died' had a special, unique significance. That the *man* Jesus *died* meant little, for many men were crucified in Jewish Palestine at that time; incomparably more astonishing was the confession that this *man* Jesus, executed as a criminal, was raised by God. To say that the Messiah had died was a complete reversal of this. It was taken for granted that God would grant victory to the Messiah; the message of his death on the cross, however, was a scandal. For in the light of all our present knowledge, the suffering and dying Messiah was not yet a familiar traditional figure in the Judaism of the first century AD. The figure of the suffering Messiah from the tribe of Ephraim only appears in the rabbinic Haggadah from about the middle of the second century AD, as a result of the catastrophes of AD 70, 115–116 and 132–135. For a Jewish audience, the confession 'the Messiah died . . .' must have been an unprecedented novelty, indeed a scandal which – at least in the light of our present knowledge of extant sources – contradicted the prevailing popular messianic expectation.

It is easy to find the fixed historical starting point for this statement about the death of the Messiah, which sounded so aggressive to a Jewish audience. In Mark's passion narrative[11] Jesus is handed over by the supreme Jewish authorities to the Roman prefect as a messianic pretender; he is condemned by Pilate on the basis of his own confession; he is mocked by the soldiers as king of the Jews, and finally crucified as such. The charge on which he is crucified, as stated on the *titulus*, together with the mockery of the leaders of the people at the crucified Messiah, is an expression of Jesus' complete human failure, which then culminates in the desperate cry from Ps. 22.2.

In recent times, attempts have been made to see the death of Jesus not so much in traditional terms, as that of the suffering messianic servant of God; instead, the widespread theme of the 'righteous sufferer' has been used to interpret the passion of Jesus, and reference has been made in this connection to the use of the psalms of suffering in the Marcan passion narrative. Here we are supposed to have a version of the pattern of the humiliation and exaltation of the innocent, of a similar kind to the one which also appears in Wisdom 2–5. A one-sided introduction of this theme, however, misinterprets the intention of the passion in Mark. The pattern of the humiliation and exaltation of the righteous is far too general and imprecise to interpret the event which Mark narrates so skilfully and with such deep theological reflection. He is concerned with the utterly unique event of the passion and crucifixion of the Messiah of Israel which is without any parallel in the history of religion. For Mark, the few psalms of suffering which illuminate individual features of the suffering and death of Jesus, like Psalms 22 and 69, are exclusively *messianic* psalms, such as Psalms 110 and 118. The 'righteous' does not appear in connection with Jesus either in the two psalms or in Mark; it is only Matthew with his rabbinic training who makes the Messiah Jesus into an exemplary *ṣaddiq*. Where features from the suffering of the righteous man appear, for example in the mocking of Jesus, they are also in a messianic key. The suffering 'of the righteous' is to be integrated completely and utterly into the suffering of the Messiah. *The Messiah alone is the righteous and sinless one par excellence.* His suffering therefore has irreplaceable and unique significance.

The category of the 'martyr prophet' is another one which is inadequate for understanding the passion of Jesus: in Mark 12.1–11 a very clear distinction is made between the unique, 'beloved' son and heir and the different servants who are sent first. The *unmessianic* interpretation of the person and work of Jesus which has become customary in Germany from the time of Wrede not only obstructs a historical and theological understanding of the emergence of the early christology of the first community, but hinders a real understanding of the passion of Jesus. At this point I can only point emphatically to N. A. Dahl, who rightly stressed that resurrection and exaltation could not by themselves serve as a justification for holding Jesus to be Messiah.[12] There was no Jewish doctrine of the appointment of a Messiah and Son of Man through the resurrection and exaltation of a dead man. The appearance of the risen Jesus is therefore in no way an adequate foundation for his messiahship and for the later development of christology, nor does it give a satisfactory explanation of them.

However, this raises in an even more basic way the question which dominates the whole of the second half of the Gospel of Mark and which cannot be answered simply by reference to the 'suffering righteous' and the 'martyr prophet'. Why does the Messiah–Son of Man have to suffer, according to God's will but in contradiction to the prevailing contemporary Jewish messianic tradition as we know it? Mark gives an adequate answer to this question in Mark 10.45, which he deliberately puts at the end of the public ministry of Jesus outside Jerusalem, and through the account of the Last Supper (14.22–25), which at the same time is the last instruction of the disciples before the passion. Here the imminent death of Jesus is interpreted in an inclusive, universal way as being 'for all men', in connection with Isa. 53 and the covenant sacrifice of Ex. 24.8 (cf. also Zech. 9.11), as a representative atoning death 'for the many'.

No one can say that this theme is completely absent from the subsequent passion account. How else could we interpret the rending of the veil of the Temple, which set apart the holy of holies, in Mark 15.38, than by saying that Jesus' death opens the way into the holy of holies, the place of atonement for the sins of Israel and of the presence of God, and robs the old cult of its force?[13] The quotation from Isa. 56.7, that the Temple is 'a house of prayer for all nations, prepares for this event, and the remark of the Gentile centurion, who is the first to utter the saving confession of faith as a representative of 'all nations' or 'the many', shows that the atonement has already become effective. Furthermore, the darkness which symbolically follows the mocking of the crucified Messiah about the sixth hour and ends with his cry of forsakenness about the ninth hour is a sign that the death of Jesus itself was understood as a saving event (Mark 15.33f., 37). It is clear from all this why the pattern of the suffering of the righteous man, which has proved so popular, is also so inadequate for contemporary theological reflection. According to Wisdom 2–5, the righteous sufferer first achieves salvation only for himself; for others he acts as a model, or is an accuser of his enemies; in essentials, this is the familiar formula of the *per aspera ad astra*, which we also find in connection with the heroes of the Greek world, and Heracles in particular.

Of course, here to a great extent we are still moving in the sphere of the theological interpretation made by Mark, who presumably wrote his gospel shortly before AD 70. The masterly arrangement of the material at least is his work, even if, as I believe, he took over a much earlier account in his passion narrative. We need to look back further to find the beginnings of the interpretation of the death of Jesus as vicarious atonement. Here a comparison between Mark and the earlier Paul can help us: Mark describes the death of Jesus as the death of the crucified Messiah. He does this with almost penetrating persistence. Between Mark 15.13 and 16.6 he uses the verb σταυροῦν, which was so offensive to ancient ears, eight times, and three times he talks of the σταυρός of the Messiah. Only those who understand how extremely offensive this word will have been to both Jewish and Gentile ears will be able to grasp what that means. Here there is no hagiographical transformation of the scandal: it is expressed openly. The twofold invitation made by the leaders of the people in Mark 15.30 and 32 to Jesus to come down from the cross contains an appeal to transform the scandalous and accursed death into triumph. This offence can still be clearly traced in the later polemic of writers like Celsus (Origen, *Contra Celsum* 2.33–37). Here we come up against the weightiest argument in anti-Christian polemic of both Jewish and Gentile origin. Through his death on the 'cursed tree' Jesus has proved to be a pitiful deceiver and his followers have proved to be dupes. In addition, Jews would inevitably understand talk of a crucified Messiah as blasphemy, because of Deut. 21.23. The Messiah of Israel could never ever at the same time be the one who according to the words of the Torah was accursed by God. It was perhaps for this very reason that the leaders of the people and their clientèle had pressed for the execution of Jesus by crucifixion.[14] This was the most obvious way to refute his messianic claim.

Although countless Jews were crucified under the Seleucids, the Hasmoneans and above all under the Romans, and although there

were so many crucified pious men and teachers, as far as I can see
we find only one reference to a crucified martyr in rabbinic sources:
Jose ben Joezer, the legendary teacher from the time of the
Maccabees.[15] Deuteronomy 21.23 evidently made it difficult to
turn a crucified man into a religious figure or a hero. For that very
reason, Paul describes his message in I Cor. 1.17, with polemical
accentuation, as λόγος τοῦ σταυροῦ; in it he means to proclaim
none other than the Χριστὸς ἐσταυρομένος, i.e. the crucified
Messiah (1.23; cf. 2.2; Gal. 3.1), who was a religious scandal to the
Jews and a delusion to the Greeks.

At this point we come back to the first question about the uniqueness of the proclamation of the universal atoning sacrifice of the
crucified Jesus (see p. 31 above). One feature of it is its unavoidable
offensiveness to ancient ears. Although they have been toned down
to suit Luke's apologetic concern, the allusions in Acts 5.30 and
10.39 show that the interpretation of the death of Jesus on the
cross as a 'curse for us' (Gal. 3.13, following Deut. 21.23) was not
just an exegetical 'discovery' of Paul's.

If we go back from the Paul of the letters to the apostle's conversion, which is to be dated only a few years after Easter, say between
AD 32 and AD 34, the decisive problem is why the young Pharisee
Sha'ul – Paul, with his scribal training, was so intensively occupied
in the persecution and destruction of the community of Christian
'Hellenists' in Jerusalem. Did they not cause offence precisely
through their blasphemous message of the crucified Messiah and
its theological consequences? In Acts 6.13, Stephen, the leader of
this group, is accused of having made attacks 'against this holy
place', i.e. the Temple, 'and the Law' (cf. 6.20; 7.48). The 'zeal'
of the persecutor (Phil. 3.6) must have been directed against these
attempts to shake the foundations of Israel's existence, indeed the
foundation of the whole of creation (Aboth 1.1). But what was the
basis of these attacks on the sanctuary and the Torah? Presumably
the certainty that the death of the crucified Messiah, who had
vicariously taken upon himself the curse of the Law, had made the
Temple obsolete as a place of everlasting atonement for the sins of
Israel, and therefore the ritual Law had lost its significance as a
necessary institution for salvation. There is a definite intrinsic

christological connection between the intentions of such different-sounding sayings as I Cor. 1.23; Mark 15.38; Acts 6.13 and Gal. 3.13.

In Phil. 3.8 the apostle says that the purpose of his radical change of life is 'to win Christ' and thus to receive the new 'righteousness from God' which is given 'through faith in Christ'. This ἵνα Χριστὸν κερδήσω primarily means the appropriation of the death of Christ in which God's righteousness is manifest as saving power. In Rom. 3.21–26 Paul describes the revelation of this righteousness and connects it very closely with the death of Jesus as a vicarious atoning sacrifice. Here we come upon linguistic allusions to the rite performed in the Holy of Holies on Yom Kippur. In his article '*hilastērion*', written more than thirty years ago, Professor Manson already said all that needed to be said about this verse, which is so hotly disputed: 'Christ crucified . . . like the mercy-seat in the Holy of Holies, . . . was the place where God's mercy was supremely manifested'.[16] Here we have one of the few instances in which Paul speaks of the death of Jesus in the categories of the Temple cult. For this he uses an earlier, stereotyped piece of tradition, perhaps because he knew that this language was understood well in Rome. He himself was no longer much concerned with this cultic vocabulary; now that his gaze was turned West, towards Rome and Spain, the cult of the Temple in Jerusalem had faded into the background, even if he had been forced to maintain a link with the church in Jerusalem for the sake of the unity of the church.

Nevertheless, elsewhere in his writings, the cultic language which interprets the death of Jesus as an atoning sacrifice still appears often, usually in relatively stereotyped formulations. This is evidently an earlier – one might say 'pre-Pauline' – linguistic tradition. The reference to the blood of Jesus shed on the cross appears not only in Rom. 3.25, in the context of the atoning sacrifice of Yom Kippur, but also in the paradosis of the Last Supper in I Cor. 11.25, as the sign of the new covenant. Underlying this is probably an interpretation of the self-sacrifice of Jesus as the sacrifice which seals the new covenant. In Romans 5.9 the blood of Jesus is the means by which justification takes place. This statement is closely connected with the preceding v. 8, in which the atoning death of Jesus 'for us, while we were still sinners', is interpreted as a sign of the love of God. The incarnate Son appears in the context of the mission statement in Rom. 8.3 as the atoning sacrifice (περὶ ἁμαρτίας = *ḥaṭṭa't*), through which God 'judges sin in the flesh'. In II Cor. 5.21, also, the statement that as the sinless one Christ was 'made sin for us' by God (τὸν μὴ γνόντα ἁμαρτίαν ὑπὲρ ἡμῶν ἁμαρτίαν ἐποίησεν) is to be understood to mean that Christ is offered on our behalf as the perfect sin offering. One might also recall I Cor. 5.7: 'Christ our passover is sacrificed', or the intercession of the heavenly high priest at the right hand of God in Rom. 8.34 and the προσαγωγή in Rom. 5.2, the essential basis of which is access to the presence of God in the heavenly sanctuary. Granted, all this does not amount to much, but the multiplicity of themes is all the more striking. Paul contents himself with the relatively frequent and brief formulae concerned with dying and 'surrendering', and remarkably enough, even the theme of the death of Jesus 'for our sins' takes a back place in comparison with the mere 'for us', on the basis of his anthropology. In addition he knows of other concept slike redemption or καταλλάσεσ-εσθαι or καταλλαγή, deriving from the sphere of interpersonal relationships, a group of words which could also of course be interpreted in a cultic sense (cf. e.g. Sophocles, *Ajax* 744: θεοῖσιν ὡς καταλλαχθῇ χόλου).

As there is a similar multiplicity of cultic terminology in individual deutero-Pauline letters, in I Peter, the Johannine corpus, Revelation, and above all Hebrews, and it is even more prominent here than it is in Paul, it seems likely that this language is not fortuitous and did not arise on the periphery of christological development, but – along with the formulae about dying and 'surrendering' – has a common root. Another indication of this is the use of the metaphor of the sacrificial lamb without blemish for the crucified and exalted Jesus, which we find attested independently in I Peter 1.19; John 1.29, 35f. and Revelation, and which is also to be presupposed in I Cor. 5.7. Underlying this is probably the interpretation of Jesus as the passover lamb, a reference which goes back to the last meal of Jesus with his disciples.

However, the one common root of all this multiple tradition is probably to be discovered where there had been a fundamental break with the atoning and saving significance of sacrifice in the worship of the Temple in Jerusalem and where the theological significance of this break – which did not come about without harsh resistance – had to be worked out. This break was explained in terms of the revolutionary insight that the death of the Messiah Jesus on Golgotha had brought about once and for all – note the significance of the ἅπαξ or ἐφάπαξ in such different texts as Rom. 6.10; I Peter 3.18 and Heb. 7.27; 9.12, etc. – universal atonement for all guilt.

(iii) The atoning death of Jesus in the earliest community

Of course this gives rise to further questions:

1. Does the universal soteriological interpretation of the death of Jesus, which necessarily led to a break with the sacrificial cult in the Temple, represent a step which was forced on the Hellenists by what was fundamentally secondary, artificial and scribal reflection compared with the elemental experience of encounter with the risen Lord, and which therefore necessarily presupposes a certain passage of time in the narrow interval which still remained? Or is the recognition of the atoning effect of the death of Jesus just as elemental for all concerned as the certainty that God raised Jesus from the dead?

2. Can we also presuppose an analogous theological insight in the Aramaic-speaking community around Peter and the Twelve? In other words, what is the status of the ultimate unity of the earliest Christian preaching which is attested to by Paul in I Cor. 15.11 and Gal. 2.7–9? Has Paul taken too much on himself here, and do we have to mistrust him?

3. Can the soteriological interpretation of the death of Jesus be derived with some degree of historical probability from the initiative of Jesus himself? Were this the case, we would essentially have answered the first two questions.

First of all a preliminary remark. Here we find a controversy in which a variety of conflicting arguments appear. It is hardly possible to arrive at real historical *certainty* in this obscure sphere of the event which gave rise to the earliest Christian community. We come across this phenomenon often in the earliest history of Christianity. A fundamental distinction must be made from the foundation of our faith. My certainty that Christ died for my guilt is neither strengthened nor attacked by the final results of this discussion over historical probabilities. There is no historical proof for the truth of faith. The certainty of faith has a different quality from historical knowledge. Here we are concerned only with the simple question: What is more probable after a careful examination of the sources? Of course, the result of this quest for what is historically most probable is not without a significance for a better theological *understanding* of the origin of earliest Christianity, its preaching and its christology.

Answering the questions raised above is also indissolubly connected with the question of the messianic claim of Jesus. If, as radical German critics maintain, Jesus never spoke of Messiah or Son of Man; if – incomprehensibly enough – he was crucified only as 'rabbi and prophet',[17] as *ḥasīd* and *ṣaddīq*, in short as a pious martyr, the appearances of the risen Jesus could be understood only as confirmation of his blameless piety, his exaltation to paradise, to the fathers resting there, and as a demonstration of the proof of his preaching about the kingdom of God, of course with the qualification that the kingdom of God which he had announced was still further delayed. True, this would have confirmed in essentials for the disciples the quite personal 'cause of Jesus' and put things straight; but they would hardly have gone on in the extremely vigorous way that they did. The case of Jesus – now exalted to God – could have been concluded satisfactorily, and the dawn of the kingdom of God could have been awaited in tranquillity. Easter, i.e. the appearances of the risen Jesus mentioned in I Cor. 15.4ff., in no way explains how the alleged 'rabbi and prophet' became the Messiah and Son of Man – which also means the exalted Lord, *maran*, of the community –, in short, how 'the proclaimer became the proclaimed'. If Jesus had no messianic features at all, the origin of the Christian kerygma would remain completely inexplicable and mysterious. In order to bridge this gap we would be reduced to yet more new and incredible hypotheses. As long as scholarship which calls itself 'critical' does not raise this historical problem properly, it does not deserve the title it bears. In the Judaism of the time there were some authoritative teachers and pious martyrs who were said to have been transported to heaven or taken into the Garden of Eden after their deaths. Not one of them was made Son of Man or Messiah. Nor do we have any indication whatsoever that a martyr prophet could be exalted to be Son of Man through resurrection from the dead. The only 'exaltation' of a man and his identification with the 'Son of Man – Messiah' which is known to us is that of Enoch (Ethiopian Enoch 71). However, he is a hero from primal times with superhuman wisdom and authority. Equally improbable is a lengthy process of tradition, i.e. spread out over a number of years, after the Easter appearances, in which the fundamental features of the primitive Christian kerygma as we find it, say, in I Cor. 15.3, gradually developed, and in which the various christological titles were slowly and successively transferred to Jesus. Here we should no longer reckon in years, but in months or even weeks, and given such short periods of time we are hardly in any position to make subtle distinctions.[18]

The decisive statements must in fact already have been formulated in Greek some time before the calling of Paul. Otherwise there would have been no uproar against Stephen and his friends in the Greek-speaking synagogues of Jerusalem. The usual chronological patterns which are used – without reference to real chronology, – 'early or late traditions', are too indefinite and really do not say anything. We have already seen that the kerygma of the Hellenists, whom Paul fought against and persecuted in Jerusalem, was based on the offensive statement: 'The Messiah died for us (our sins).' Now this formula of 'dying for' (ἀποθνῄσκειν ὑπέρ) is striking because it has no parallel in the Old Testament and the Semitic sphere, though it is frequent in Greek texts, not least those of Hellenistic Jewish provenance from the time of the Maccabees. In contrast to this, the surrender formula clearly goes back to a Semitic basis, as is clear above all from its earliest formulation in the tradition, in Mark 10.45.[19] The formula *nātan* or *māsar napšō ʿal* (δοῦναι τὴν ψυχὴν αὐτοῦ ὑπέρ) is variously attested in later Hebrew texts. There is also a Hebraism – presumably from Isa. 53 – in the inclusive, universal significance of πολλοί = *rabbīm* in the sense of πάντες, and the λύτρον ἀντί corresponds with the Hebrew *kōfer taḥat*, which probably goes back to Isa. 43.3f.[20] Thus both formulae, that of the dying of the Messiah and the surrender formula, have different derivations in the history of the tradition.

The Hellenists in Jerusalem, who for the first time recast the primitive Christian message (and the tradition of Jesus) in the Greek language, were linguistically creative in many respects. It is to them that 'we are presumably indebted for the new and specifically Christian meaning of εὐαγγέλιον, εὐαγγελίζεσθαι; ἀπόστολος, ἐκκλησία, κοινωνία, παρουσία, χάρις, πίστις, ἀποκάλυψις, ἀπολύτρωσις, πρὸ (ἀπὸ) καταβολῆς κόσμου, and so on, and even the phrase ὁ υἱὸς τοῦ ἀνθρώπου (instead of the υἱὸς ἀνθρώπου of the LXX), so mysterious because it has the definite article. We may regard this hermeneutically significant and effective work of translation as a fruit of the enthusiastic experience of the Spirit which came about in the earliest community. The new message was also to be proclaimed to the Jews and godfearers in Jerusalem, the coastal regions of Palestine and the cities of Phoenicia and Syria, indeed to the Diaspora generally, many of whom only spoke Greek. What is more likely than to suppose that the formula Χριστὸς ἀπέθανεν ὑπὲρ (τῶν ἁμαρτιῶν) ἡμῶν, which is pre-Pauline in the full sense of the word, was formed in connection with this creative translation of the new kerygma into Greek? Possibly it was meant to counter statements in the LXX which reject a 'dying for others' (cf. Deut. 24.16; Jer. 38 (31).30; Ezek. 3.18f.; 18.4ff.): the death of the Messiah creates the possibility of representativeness.

Of course this would rule out another obvious possibility. The LXX very often uses the phrase ἐξιλάσκεσθαι περί to translate the Hebrew *kipper 'al*, referring either to people (or pronouns) or to their sins. So here too we find shorter and longer forms (e.g. περὶ ὑμῶν or περὶ τῶν ἁμαρτιῶν ὑμῶν) side by side, with very little difference between them. That this terminology, which makes use of the root ἱλασκ-, also had a certain, albeit limited influence on the soteriological interpretation of the death of Jesus, is shown not only by Rom. 3.25 and Heb. 2.7, but above all by I John, where Christ is twice described as ἱλασμὸς περὶ τῶν ἁμαρτιῶν ἡμῶν (cf. 2.2; 4.10).

This terminology was more directly related to the atoning sacrificial cult of the Temple than the very Greek-sounding formulae of Paul and – as I would suggest – the Hellenists. It is easy to explain why this not directly cultic, Graecized formula was preferred to that of the LXX, which was more connected with the Jerusalem cult: the formula Χριστὸς ἀπέθανεν ὑπέρ . . . expressed the uniqueness of the death of Jesus and its soteriological significance over against the constant atoning sacrifices in the Temple; in contrast to the universal atoning effect of the death of Jesus these latter only had a very limited force and therefore had to be repeated constantly. Presumably the verb *kipper* = ἐξιλάσκεσθαι was too closely associated with the idea of the ever new sacrificial acts of atonement in the cult. By contrast, 'the Messiah died for us' expressed clearly the ἐφάπαξ of reconciliation (Rom. 6.10). The rabbinic tradition, which deliberately restricts the effect of Yom Kippur in a number of ways, rests on an earlier tradition which goes back to the Second Temple. Whereas there, for example, atonement is divided into the three components of conversion, Yom Kippur and man's own death (M. Yoma 8.8 etc.), in the death of Jesus the effective atonement which guaranteed salvation was concentrated on one point: the death of the Messiah on the cross. All purely human action had to fade into the background in the face of that. Paul's idea, which he also assumes the Roman Christians to have heard of, that in the death of Jesus all have died, has its ultimate foundation here (II Cor. 5.14f.; cf. Rom. 6.3f.).

By means of the new kerygmatic formula of the saving significance of the death of the Messiah, the Hellenists stressed the radical newness of the once-and-for-all, eschatological atonement which had taken place on Golgotha, which had been made manifest by the resurrection of Jesus, and now had to be proclaimed to all men. Thus the formula represented a demarcation from the worship of the Temple, which expressed the fundamental, qualitative difference between the dying of Jesus on the cross on Golgotha and the ongoing sin-offerings on Mount Zion. If one so desired, one might say that the atonement achieved through Christ developed its saving power directly, in the heavenly sanctuary, and not just on the altar and in the earthly Holy of Holies. In this way access to the direct presence of God himself had been opened up for the believer.

There are several independent references which tend in this direction: 'For through him we . . . have access (τὴν προσαγωγήν) to the Father' (Eph. 2.18; cf. 3.12; Rom. 5.2). Through the self-sacrifice of the true high priest Jesus we are enabled to 'draw near with confidence to the throne of grace, that we may receive mercy . . .' (Heb. 4.16). We find similar formulae in a christological hymn (I Peter 3.18):

> For Christ also suffered for sins once for all,
> the righteous for the unrighteous,
> that he might bring you to God
> (ἵνα ὑμᾶς προσαγάγῃ τῷ θεῷ).

Behind all these different statements lies an older common tradition.

Nevertheless, the Temple on Mount Zion had not yet lost all its functions; instead of being a place of sacrifice it was a 'house of prayer for all nations'; as one might say, it had become the universal centre of all synagogues. Taking over the familiar formula ἐξιλάσκεσθαι περί from the LXX had furthered the misunderstanding that in fact the death of Jesus was only as important as Temple worship, and stood alongside it; it could not represent the eschatological superseding and abolition of it. In the last resort this is the reason for the astonishing predominance of the preposition ὑπέρ as an expression of the saving efficacy of the death of Jesus in the New Testament texts, as opposed to περί made more familiar through the LXX as a translation of the Hebrew 'al.

Nevertheless, alongside this, Old Testament references to sacrifice – and indeed an astonishing number and variety of them – were applied to the death of Jesus. This is connected on the one hand with the obvious analogy which it provided, but even more with *the consistent eschatological and christological proof from scripture.* As the Old Testament writings were written as τύποι for the eschatological present (I Cor. 10.11; Rom. 15.4), what they say about sacrifice – understood in the right way – must point beyond them to their eschatological fulfilment in Christ. Atonement through the Temple cult finds its *end and* at the same time also its *fulfilment* in the eschatological saving event on Golgotha. This multiple reference, which expresses both the actual difference between Temple worship and the death of Jesus, together with the analogy between them and an eschatological typology, explains the remarkable fact that in the New Testament texts from Paul to the Johannine corpus the death of Jesus is interpreted, not all that often, but unmistakably and in constantly changing ways, in analogy to the Temple cult. The basis for the multiplicity of these descriptions – very like that of the christological titles – lies in the deliberately chosen 'multiplicity of approaches'.

However, our investigation into origins goes further. Can the soteriological interpretation of the death of Jesus be traced back with some degree of probability only as far as the 'Hellenists', so that we have to suppose that they were the first to express this central idea of the primitive Christian kerygma – under the creative impulse of the *Spirit* – or are there indications which might lead us to look for the origin of this expression of faith in the primal event which brought the church into being?

I have already referred to one of them. As we find it in Mark 10.45, the surrender formula indicates an original Semitic form which must come either from the Aramaic-speaking community or from Jesus himself. A further starting point is the *Lord's Supper*. Both the paradosis in I Cor. 11.23–25, where Paul refers to a historical event with a specific date, and the account in Mark 14. 22–25, contain the interpretation of the death of Jesus as an atoning saving event. In its oldest demonstrable form it is specially bound up with the cup of wine at the Last Supper, and similarly goes back to the Jerusalem community. For in all probability the interpretation of the death of Jesus as a covenant sacrifice along the lines of Ex. 24.8, which is presupposed in the word over the cup in Mark 14.24, and which the (pre-)Pauline tradition expands with a reference to the new covenant of Jer. 31.31, is already to be presupposed in Palestine, since the ' rgumim (Onkelos and Yerushalmi I)

expressly speak of the atoning effect of the blood rite in the covenant sacrifice of Ex. 24.8, and Mark's version with its Semitic-type
formula τοῦτό ἐστιν τὸ αἷμά μου τῆς διαθήκης τὸ ἐκχυννόμενον
ὑπὲρ πολλῶν also presupposes such an atoning understanding of
the death of Jesus as an eschatological covenant sacrifice.[21] By contrast, the earliest accounts of the Supper in Paul and Mark have no
connection whatsoever with ancient memorial meals for the dead
or mystery celebrations. This is even truer of the pre-Pauline
celebration of the Lord's Supper in the earliest community.

Finally and in conclusion one can also hardly imagine how the
unity of the earliest church – so dear to Paul's heart – could have
been preserved had the community in Jerusalem not shared this
belief in the soteriological efficacy of the death of Jesus. In view of
the daily sacrifice in the Temple, the question whether atonement
took place there or whether God himself had 'finally' brought it
about through the crucifixion of the Messiah must have become
even more urgent.

How can Paul – with relatively few exceptions – content himself
with formulae and not explain in detail the atoning death of the
Messiah 'for us'? The reason is probably that the 'that' in this
formula was in no way controversial, even in Galatia and in the
Roman church which was unknown to him; the problems lay in
the soteriological consequences, say in connection with the ongoing importance of the Torah and the works which it required.
Paul had thought through radically to the end the consequences of
the saving significance of the death of Jesus which the Hellenists
had already sketched out; however, the substance does not derive
first from him nor from the Hellenists – its roots lie deeper.

For example, it is striking that two writings which according to
the tradition of the early church – in my view completely reliable –
must be assigned to the Petrine sphere of tradition, Mark and I
Peter, stress the soteriological interpretation of the death of Jesus
as an atoning death in a marked way, I Peter by an explicit citation
of Isa. 53 (2.17ff.; 3.18f.; cf. 1.18), and Mark in two places in an
archaic Semitic linguistic form. We know very little indeed about
the work of Peter as leader of the Jerusalem community and later
as a missionary. If we assume – and this is still the most likely

thing – that he was executed in Rome during Nero's persecution in AD 64, his activity extended over a period of thirty-four years; it is longer than that of Paul. That it was not without effect is clear from the letters to the Corinthians – despite Paul's vigorous remark in I Cor. 15.10: ἀλλὰ περισσότερον αὐτῶν πάντων ἐκοπίασα, where Paul had to fight against what for him was the threat posed by the Petrine mission – and also from Gal. 1 and 2. We can hardly doubt that Peter had a special theological authority within the first generation of earliest Christian history, and also in the Pauline missionary communities, even if today people sometimes talk about earliest Christianity as though Peter had never existed. The conclusion follows almost of necessity: the Petrine kerygma, too, must have known and shared as its central content the atoning death of Jesus. Otherwise in Antioch Paul would not have been able to argue polemically against it at all, since there would not have been the basic presuppositions for any argument. At first, Peter too 'lived like a Gentile' in Antioch (Gal. 2.14): for him also Christ and not the Torah must have been the foundation of revelation. Conversely, it is hardly credible that the greatest authority of the earliest Christian period could have taken over this central confession at some later stage from the Hellenists – expelled from Jerusalem because of their polemic against the Temple – or invented it on his own authority. If anywhere, its roots must be inseparably bound up with the foundation of his experience of faith.

(iv) Historical and traditio-historical objections

Of course, various objections could be made to this:

1. First, the Temple cult and the legal regulations associated with it still seem to have had some significance for the *Jewish Christians in Judaea*. That can be inferred from James' invitation to Paul to undertake the discharge of Nazirite vows, the tradition of texts from Jesus like Matt. 5.23f., and Luke's notes about the acceptance of priests and zealous Pharisees. On the other hand, we hear from Paul (I Thess. 2.14; cf. Gal. 1.22) that it was the communities in Judaea in particular which were persecuted by the

Jewish authorities, evidently even after the expulsion of the Hellenists. According to Luke, the Sadducean priestly nobility were the main driving force here; a later wave of persecution was caused by king Agrippa I (AD 40–44; Acts 12). In AD 62, the chief Sadducee and then high priest, Annas, son of the Annas of the passion narrative, had James the brother of the Lord and other Jewish Christians stoned for breaking the Law.[22] According to the apocryphal *anabathmoi Iakobou*, James is said to have attacked 'the Temple, sacrifice and the altar fire';[23] the Pseudo-Clementines, which are influenced by Jewish Christianity, also rejected the sacrificial cult.[24] The conjecture made by H. J. Schoeps that the rejection of sacrifice by the Ebionites also makes a soteriological interpretation of the death of Jesus in the earliest Palestinian community improbable, is untenable; the opposite is the case. The death of Jesus was presumably one of the causes of the Ebionite criticism of sacrifice, even if this is no longer clear from the late traditions of the third and fourth centuries.[25] The constant opposition of the Sadducean priestly nobility to the Jewish Christians could best be explained by a permanently critical attitude towards the sacrificial cult on their part. In my view, it is therefore probable that from the beginning the Jewish Christians adopted a fundamentally detached attitude to the cult, but were prepared for certain compromises on account of the world in which they lived. Even the Essenes, who rejected the real cult in Jerusalem, were ready to honour the Temple with dedicated gifts (ἀναθήματα).[26] We have no indication whatsoever that the Jewish Christians in Judaea felt an unconditional obligation to worship on Mount Zion; on the contrary, there is some evidence that they had a somewhat broken relationship with it, but had to show a certain compliance if they were to remain in existence. In my view this is also clear from the tradition about the Temple tax underlying Matt. 17.24–27, which probably came into being some time before AD 70, since after the destruction of the Temple the half-shekel tax had to be paid as a *fiscus Judaicus* in Rome to the temple of Juppiter Capitolinus. There Jesus stresses to Simon Peter that as sons of God they are free from the Temple tax, but that they should nevertheless pay it in order to avoid any offence. This rejection of the traditional cult must have had very early roots, as it tended to be weakened under external pressure in the later decades down to AD 70. The best explanation of it is that Jewish Christians in their Palestinian homeland also maintained the fundamental saving significance of the death of Jesus as the sinless Messiah, and no longer ascribed atoning effect to sacrifice in the sanctuary. The special stress on Hos. 6.6 in Matt. 9.13; 12.7 probably derives from Jewish-Christian theology. Hosea 6.6 is cited again in the pseudo-Clementine *Recognitions*, 1.37.2. The legendary account of Hegesippus in Eusebius, about the constant prayer of the Lord's brother in the Temple, does not tell against this. Precisely because the Temple no longer served as a place of sacrifice and atonement, but had become 'a house of prayer' (Mark 11.17–Isa. 56.7), the tradition could develop that James went alone to the Temple and there 'constantly went down on his knees to pray to God and ask him for forgiveness for his people'.[27] He, James, the brother of Jesus, as earthly intercessor for disobedient Israel, corresponded to Jesus the Son of Man as the heavenly intercessor at the right hand of God. By contrast, the Temple cult itself had lost its atoning effect.

The following objections are more difficult to answer. Here we have a traditio-historical problem. *In Aramaic-speaking Jewish Palestine, round about the year AD 30, could the notion of the universal representative atonement achieved by the death of the Messiah come into being at all?* A number of counter-arguments are advanced against this possibility.

2. *Inter alia*, these include the history of *the influence of Isa. 53*, the only Old Testament text which could have prompted the beginning of this development, as elsewhere the Old Testament tends to reject vicarious atonement or the death of a man for the sins of others (see above, p. 7). However, at this particular point one would be glad of a substantiated history of interpretation in the pre-Christian period. One would not refer, either, to the messianic interpretation of this chapter in the prophetic Targum, as this is post-Christian, and in it not only are the statements about suffering transferred to the nations and thus turned into statements about salvation for Israel, but the idea of vicarious suffering is interpreted away. I myself feel that an 'anti-Christian' interpretation is

quite probable, though there is no sure proof of this and as a result it will always be a matter for dispute.[28] The only 'remnant' to which reference could be made is the Armenian version of TestBenj 3, which contains an earlier version of the vicarious suffering of a sinless man probably without Christian interpolations. However, even here there is dispute over the messianic interpretation and the originality of the text.[29] On the other hand, however, it must be recognized that with the exception of PsSol 17 and 18, we have very few 'messianic' texts from the pre-Christian period in any case, and therefore do not know very much about Jewish messianic expectations before the Christian era. There was certainly not a fixed 'doctrine of the Messiah' before the first century AD. It would be therefore better to talk of a plurality of messianic motifs.[30] It should also be noted that the LXX translation, which already diverges strongly from the Hebrew text, represents a quite arbitrary 'interpretation', which shows that this text was not without effect in pre-Christian times. The same is true of Aquila, Theodotion, Symmachus and the Targum, even though they are post-Christian. Even rabbinic interpretation is not uninteresting, and refers the text both to the Messiah and to the innocent sufferer. There was evidently constant work on and with this refractory text.[31] Furthermore, J. Starcky has already pointed to an Aramaic text which presumably comes from a Testament of Jacob, in which there is mention of an eschatological saviour figure who 'achieves atonement for all the sons of his race', who 'teaches the will of God' and whose word 'works to the ends of the earth'. However, he comes up against resistance and enmity, 'and is involved in deceit and violence'.[32] Abbé Starcky, who kindly put this text at my disposal, also told me that in a further fragment of the same writing and perhaps even in the same column, there is mention of a persecuted person. *wmk'byn 'l* appears in the first line; *ngdy mk'bykh* is all that is left of the third. As *mak'ob*, which is relatively rare in the Old Testament, appears twice in close succession in Isa. 53.3 and 4, there could well be a reference to this chapter here. The servant of God is indeed the 'man of sorrows'. However, we cannot of course reach certainty here. Our knowledge is indeed 'in part', and we must be content with the fragment of old documents

which worms and beetles have left to us. Of course this 'not know-
ing' also holds for the opposite position. We cannot claim that Isa.
53 had no kind of messianic interpretation in pre-Christian
Judaism.[33] It is simply the case that too few texts have come down
to us from the pre-rabbinic period. Think of the treasures which
the library of Qumran, with its thousand scrolls, may have con-
tained, and of the tiny fragment which has come down to us! Of
the Isaiah *pesharim* we sadly know only parts of the passage on
Isa. 11, and nothing on Isa. 53. The fact that the first Isaiah scroll
from Cave 1 read *mšḥty* (i.e. *māšaḥtî*, cf. Isa. 61.1), instead of the
mysterious word *mšḥt* (*mišḥat* or *mošḥat*), could equally indicate a
messianic interpretation, though it probably stems from a scribal
error.

So far, then, we have no clear text from pre-Christian Judaism
which speaks of the vicarious suffering of the Messiah in connection with Isa. 53. Of course, this does not rule out the possibility
of such a tradition, and there are some indications in favour of it,
but the basis provided by our sources is too restricted. At all events,
a suffering Messiah did not belong to the widespread popular
Messianic hope in the time of Jesus and a crucified Messiah
was a real blasphemy.

On the other hand, we must ask whether at present too much
weight is not being attached to the traditio-historical argument,
since we must reckon with creative innovations in the earliest
Christian community, which was utterly influenced by an enthusiastic and eschatological experience of the Spirit. These revolutionary innovations already began, after all, with Jesus himself.

3. By contrast, it should no longer be doubted *that Isa. 53 had
an influence on the origin and shaping of the earliest kerygma.* It was
perhaps an understandable reaction that after long and excessive
emphasis on the theme of the servant of God in the sayings of
Jesus himself, to some extent as a counterblast, people should have
wanted suddenly to drive the *'ebed Yahweh* out of large areas of
the New Testament 'with swords and staves'. However, this can
only be done by treating the texts violently.[34] Neither the formula
of the 'surrender' of Jesus nor that of his representative dying 'for
many' or 'for us' would have come into being without the back-

ground of this mysterious prophecy.[35] It must also be said that alongside the earliest 'messianic hymns', the Psalms, Isaiah was by far the most important prophetic text for Jesus and earliest Christianity. One cannot immediately measure the influence of an Old Testament text on early Christian traditions by the total of literal quotations from it, otherwise for example Hos. 6.2, which people are fond of using to explain the third day in I Cor. 15.4, would have no significance at all, as it is quoted for the first time in Tertullian (*adversus Iudaeos* 13,23; *adversus Marcionem* 4,43,1). Besides, a glance at the *loci citati et allegati ex vetere testamento* in the new Nestle-Aland[36] shows that the immediately demonstrable influence of this disputed text is by no means small: at any rate, there are ten literal quotations from the fifteen verses of Isa. 52. 13–53.12, and thirty-two allusions to it. As far as I can see, this is one of the best results for any Old Testament text to be found in the New Testament. Besides, even today we know of texts and quotations which are so very familiar to everyone that we have hesitations about continually quoting them, which would become tedious, and therefore content ourselves with allusions. This may also have been the case with so important a text for the New Testament kerygma as Isa. 53.

4. A further argument for a Hellenistic Jewish-Christian derivation of the conception of the representative atoning death of Jesus is seen in the fact that we seem to find pre-Christian references to the *vicarious atoning effect of the death of a martyr* only in Jewish Hellenistic texts.[37] These are only hinted at in II Macc. 7.32f., 37f.; the idea of representation is expressed more clearly in IV Maccabees, with its stronger Greek tone, decked out in the style of a Hellenistic panegyric, which probably comes from the Jewish community of the Antioch of the first (or second) century AD. That is the case in the prayer of Eleazar in 6.28f. and the closing considerations in 17.21f.[38] However, can we draw a distinction between 'Hellenistic' and 'Palestinian' Judaism so sharply? I have already tried to show on pp. 2f. above that this is no longer possible on the basis of our present knowledge of the sources. In addition, both II and IV Maccabees contain numerous 'Palestinian' traditions. Against this, too, is the fact that in writings composed in Palestine

we find at least beginnings in this direction. There is a penitential prayer which probably comes from the time of the Maccabean troubles; it was originally composed in Hebrew and inserted by an unknown author into the Greek additions to Daniel, where according to LXX it was spoken by all three men in the burning fiery furnace, whereas Theodotion puts it only in the mouth of Azariah.[39] This prayer first confesses that God has inflicted judgment on the people 'for our sins', that he has 'given us over into the hands of our lawless enemies and the hated apostates'; however, there follows the petition for mercy because of the merits of the patriarchs, i.e. Abraham, Isaac and Israel. In a similar way, according to the 'Hellenistic' LXX of Job and the 'Palestinian' Targum of Job from Cave 11, God forgives Job's friends their sins 'for Job's sake', that is, because of his intercession and the sacrifice which – in contrast to M – he offers for his friends.[40] At the end of the Prayer of Azariah it is stressed that because of the destruction of the Temple no further sacrifices can be offered 'to find mercy'. Instead, the suppliant prays that they may be accepted 'with a lowly spirit',

> like holocausts of rams and bulls,
> like ten thousand fat sheep,
> so may our sacrifice be before you today,
> to bring about atonement with you
> (καὶ ἐξιλάσαι ὄπισθέν σου   LXX).[41]

In the original version of the penitential prayer, the atoning sacrifice may have referred to the prayer itself, but in the mouths of the three men in the burning fiery furnace, i.e. according to the LXX version, the martyrdom of the three men becomes an atoning sacrifice offered to God. According to Dan. 3.28 'they offered up their bodies' so as not to be able to venerate any god other than the God of Israel (see above, p. 12). Here we have the earliest account of a martyrdom, from pre-Maccabean Judaism, which, however, ends with the miracle of God's deliverance. For later rabbinic tradition, despite their miraculous deliverance, the three become prototypes of the pious martyr.

5. A further complex, the age of which is disputed, is the *'Aqēdat Yiṣḥaq*, 'the binding of Isaac for sacrifice', according to

Gen. 22.[42] In rabbinic texts from the second century it provides vicarious atonement for the sins of all Israel. However, individual traces point back to an earlier period. This is the case, *inter alia*, with the identification of Mount Moriah with Mount Zion and the dating of the sacrifice of Isaac on the feast of the passover in the book of Jubilees (18.7, 13; cf. 17.15). Later, there are many references to the sacrificing of Isaac in the Pseudo-Philonic *Liber Antiquitatum Biblicarum*, which was composed towards the end of the first century AD. It has a unique significance here. First of all Isaac compares himself with the lamb which is chosen *in oblationes domini*, viz., with the sacrificial animals which are offered *pro iniquitatibus hominum*. However, as man he is destined 'to inherit the world'. There follows a prophecy: 'But my blessedness (*beatitudo*, here in the sense of blessing?) will be over all men (or also, will come to all men?), because there will be no other (sc. sacrifice), and generations will be told about me, and through me peoples will come to know that God has thought the soul of a man worthy of sacrifice.'[43]

In another passage Jephthah's daughter, also destined to be a sacrifice as a result of her father's oversight, compares herself with Isaac. She is afraid that – in contrast to his sacrifice – the sacrifice of her life will not be well-pleasing to God because of her father's hasty vow, but God himself determines 'that her life is surrendered because of his vow (cf. 39.11) and that her death will for all time be precious in my eyes'.[44]

There is a further instance in the oracle of Balaam, where it is said of Isaac: 'And because he did not object, his sacrifice was well pleasing to me, and on the basis of his blood I chose these people.'[45] There is a clear statement here of the vicarious saving effect of the sacrifice of Isaac. The connection between the sacrifice (*oblatio*) of Isaac and his blood (*pro sanguine eius*) indicates its character as an atoning sacrifice. The blood of Isaac's sacrifice is already associated with that of the passover lamb in the Tannaitic Midrash Mekilta on Exodus.[46]

The reason why by contrast the conception of atonement for the sin of Israel still does not appear explicitly may be that here attention is focussed on the future of Israel, and its election and future greatness stand in the foreground. Among other things, the allusion in Rom. 8.32 suggests that in the first century AD the soteriological interpretation of the sacrifice of Isaac was already known in Judaism.

6. We cannot go any further here in detail into the complicated question of representative atonement in the rabbinic literature, which deserves a separate monograph. Moreover, it has been dealt · with in Lohse's study, which is still a basic work.[47] We should not put too much stress on the argument that haggadic traditions about it only appear during the course of the second century, since the haggadic tradition from first-century teachers which has come down to us is relatively slim. This is already evident from a look at Bacher's *Haggadah of the Tannaites*.[48] Even more than the Halakah, the Haggadah represents a continuous broad stream in which there are constant ebbs and flows; we can see only a tiny part of this broad stream as early as the first century AD, but that certainly does not mean that the stream was not flowing then. So if a Haggadah appears for the first time in the work of a teacher from the middle of the second century, we cannot simply assert that in all probability it was not yet present in the first. In particular because of the number of political martyrs and the widespread political radicalism, even in Pharisaic circles, in the first and second centuries, the rabbinic tradition later underwent a process of strict self-censorship. In an exegesis of I Kings 20.42 and 22.34, a statement has been handed down about Shimeon b. Yohai, hostile to Rome and almost a zealot, who survived the persecution of Hadrian: 'Every drop (of blood) which flowed from that righteous man (I Kings 20.37: one of the prophet's disciples) brought about atonement for all Israel.'[49] For Shimeon b. Yohai, this was certainly not a completely new idea, but a conception which has its *Sitz im Leben* in the bloody conflict between Rome during the first century and the first half of the second. The same is true of the anonymous tradition of the Tannaitic Midrash Sifre Deut. 32.32:[50] 'the Israelites killed by the Gentiles are an expiation for the world to come' and of a whole series of statements from another Tannaitic Midrash, Mekilta Ex., e.g. on 12.1, where R. Jonathan, a contemporary of Shimeon b. Yohai, draws the further conclusion from Jonah's readiness to

sacrifice his life to save the ship (Jonah 1.12),[51] 'and so you find that the patriarchs and prophets gave their life for Israel.' The connection between Num. 25.13 and Isa. 53.12 probably also goes back to old zealot tradition: God's blessing on the zeal of Phinehas is explained by Isa. 53.12: 'because he gave up his life to death'. Thus he not only wrought atonement at that time, 'but he stands (continually) and achieves atonement until the dead are raised.'[52] In zeal for God Phinehas puts his life at risk, and as in the '*Aqēdat Yiṣhaq*, an atoning effect is ascribed to this action which goes beyond time. The doctrine of the three or four kinds of atonement: through penitence, through the Day of Atonement, through death and through suffering, already mentioned above, which is to be found in the Mishnah, Tosephta and the early Tannaitic discussion, also presupposes a lengthy development of tradition and a very complex doctrine of the various kinds of atonement, from which vicarious atonement is not excluded. The popular formula 'I will be atonement for you', which expressed solidarity with the person or persons affected by showing a readiness to take over suffering in cases of sorrow or disaster, certainly goes back to the time of the Second Temple; it later became a common cliché. It occurs often in the Mishnah and Tosephta in anecdotes which are set in a time when the Second Temple was still standing.[53] The discussion of rabbinic texts by Wengst is quite inadequate, and his criticism of E. Lohse, *Märtyrer und Gottesknecht*, suffers from his inability to cope properly with rabbinic texts.[54]

As a result, after careful consideration of all the sources indicated, we must agree with Jeremias and Lohse that the vicarious atoning effect of the death or even the suffering of a righteous man was not unknown in the Palestinian Judaism of the first century AD, independently of the question of terminology. Objections against deriving the soteriological interpretation of the death of Jesus from the earliest Aramaic-speaking community are therefore at any rate unconvincing. There is nothing from a historical or traditio-historical point of view which stands in the way of our deriving it from the earliest community and perhaps even from Jesus himself. This does not rule out the possibility *that the earliest Christian message of the self-offering of the Messiah Jesus on the cross for the*

salvation of the 'many' was an unprecedentedly new and bold – and
at the same time offensive – statement in the context of the tradition
of both Greek-speaking and Aramaic-speaking Judaism, because of
its scandalous content, its eschatological radicalism and its universal
significance.

(v) The origin of the message of the atoning death of the Messiah
Jesus
With some degree of probability, we can derive the message of the
saving death of the Messiah Jesus of Nazareth as an 'expiatory
sacrifice' for our sins from the 'basic event which gave rise to the
Christian community', and which is so difficult for us to
discern.

In this case, however, what is the relationship between this and
the events of the resurrection, along with the confession of the
resurrection to which they led? The appearances of the risen Christ
gave the disciples, utterly overwhelmed and disoriented as a result
of the shameful and accursed death of their messianic Master, the
assurance that God himself had recognized Jesus of Nazareth,
executed as a false claimant to messiahship, as the true Messiah of
Israel. The earliest confession of the resurrection, 'God has raised
Jesus from the dead', was constructed on the basis of this experience, probably following the divine predicates in the Eighteen
Benedictions, which in the second petition address God as *meqīm*
metim (Staerk, 11, Palestinian Version).[55] However, this experience
really meant much more than just the assurance that Jesus had
now been 'accepted' by God as a prophetic martyr or an innocent
sufferer in a particularly ostentatious way and had been transported into the heavenly dwellings of the righteous, along the lines
of what we find, say, in the two prophets raised from death in
Rev. 11.11f. or the children of Job in *Test. Iobi* 39.8–40.4.[56] For
the disciples, their encounters with the risen Lord first confirmed
the messianic claim of Jesus which had brought him to the cross,
a confirmation given by God himself which at the same time
amounted to his now public identification with the Son of Man,
exalted to the right hand of God (Ps. 110.1)[57] and soon to come as
judge. At the same time, through the resurrection God had proved

him to be the only innocent one, 'who knew no sin' (II Cor. 5.21).

We can hardly envisage these first days, weeks and months of the disciples after Easter as the meditative assembly of a quietistic group[58] with esoteric mystical experiences; rather, what they experienced ought to be compared with the violent force of an explosion which broke up all traditional conventions and bourgeois assurances. Here something new and unheard-of emerged, a new experience which radically transcended the everyday life of Palestinian fishermen, peasants and craftsmen. To some degree people lived with an enthusiastic assurance that the heavens would open and the kingdom of God would dawn. It was no accident that the appearances of the risen Jesus were connected with the eschatological experience of the Spirit which was compared with the force of heavenly fire. At the same time that means that the Jesus community which first took shape after Easter understood these events as the beginning of the end of the world and the dawn of the rule of God. The resurrection marked the beginning of the general resurrection of the dead; in Paul Jesus still appears as the 'firstfruits of those who have fallen asleep' (I Cor. 15.20), and in the Colossians hymn and in Revelation as the 'firstborn from the dead' (Col. 1.18; Rev. 1.5). It was hoped that believers would be made like him when he appeared (Rom. 8.29; Phil. 3.21; cf. I Thess. 4.17f.).

Jesus' preaching about the coming Son of Man was now transformed in the light of the Easter experience into the kerygma of the Lord of the community, risen, exalted to the right hand of God, and still to come, and to some extent the rule of God and his anointed were already present in embryo form. The disciples understood themselves to be the eschatological remnant of Israel and thus at the same time the nucleus of the new people of God. They were aware that they had been sent by the risen Lord himself to call their brothers to believe in the one who was exalted and still to come. In all this the dynamic and creative enthusiasm of the Spirit, as the eschatological gift of God to his renewed people, was at work. A vision of the risen Lord along with the gift of the Spirit formed the presupposition for the sending of the 'messengers of the Messiah', the ἀπόστολοι Χριστοῦ. Even for Paul, his authentication as an apostle of Jesus Christ is still inseparably bound up with the vision of the Kyrios (I Cor. 9.1; 15.8ff.).

At the same time, however, we should not overlook the humanly insuperable barrier which divided the disciples from their master. Between the kingdom of God breaking in with the resurrection and exaltation of the Messiah Jesus and the former disciples and followers of Jesus was the awareness of their *utter failure and deep guilt*. Again, it is Mark's passion which depicts everyone's guilt over God's anointed in an impressive way. This solidarity in sin unites all those involved here. No one is excepted, from Pilate and the soldiers in the execution squad, through the leaders of the people and the crowd which they goaded on, to the twelve, with Judas who betrayed Jesus and Peter who denied him, indeed to the women at the tomb who fled in utter confusion and in their fear failed to obey the command of the angel (Mark 16.8). Their flight is matched by the flight of the disciples in 14.50; thus they too share in the scandal which Jesus prophesied in Mark 14.27.[59] In this way Mark brings the crucified Messiah face to face with the barriers of human guilt. Here we can really say with Paul in Rom. 3.23, 'for all have sinned and come short of the glory of God'.

However, the question of guilt and forgiveness in the face of the imminent kingdom of God goes back even further. Repentance and the forgiveness of sins through baptism in the Jordan were proclaimed to be the only way of escaping the threat of the wrath of God to come or the fiery judgment of the coming Son of man in the revival movement, aimed at penitence, led by John the Baptist, the milieu from which Jesus himself was called to messianic service (Matt. 3.11f.; Luke 3.16f. Q) and from which the first disciples also came (John 1.35ff.). Differing somewhat from the preaching of John the Baptist, by both his words and his deeds Jesus himself had proclaimed the boundless love of the Father for all who were lost, and had himself promised forgiveness to individual sinners. The forgiveness of sins had been an essential ingredient of the Lord's Prayer: the coming of the kingdom and the removal of sin were indissolubly connected.

John the Baptist apparently failed in his preaching of repentance and his baptism in the Jordan, and was executed as a martyr prophet. Jesus, too, came up against growing rejection and resistance with his message of the dawn of the kingdom of God and the overwhelming love of the Father, above all among those of his contemporaries who had influence and power. In other words, the guilt of the leaders of the people and their followers in Jerusalem, like that of the disciples, was bound up with the guilt of the whole people. They resisted the coming of the kingdom of God. This means, with the passion and the death of Jesus the question of guilt became more oppressive and more urgent than ever, and no one could avoid it: the appearances of the risen Jesus gave it new and added urgency.

Another factor makes it clear that the earliest community put at the heart of their proclamation the problem of the forgiveness of sins, which was central for both John the Baptist and for Jesus. Indeed, in this respect the original church can in some ways be regarded as the heir and instrument of the 'revival movement' which came into being with John the Baptist. Peter and the Twelve once again made baptism 'for the forgiveness of sins' binding as an 'eschatological sacrament' or as a 'sealing' for the coming kingdom of God and his Messiah, albeit now 'in the name of the Messiah Jesus' (Acts 2.38, cf. 3.19), in order to express its dedication to the guarantor of salvation. This reintroduction of baptism 'for the forgiveness of sins' during the earliest period in Palestine itself – presumably under the impulse of the Spirit – for its part presupposes the insight that the eschatological event of the death of Jesus 'for us' had atoned for past sin and created 'peace with God'. According to Mek. Ex. 20.25,[60] 'peace between the Israelites and their Father in heaven' was brought about on the altar. Now at the end of the old age and the dawn of the new, the crucified Messiah had appeared once and for all to replace this constant occurrence. At the same time this certainty answered the urgent question why the Messiah had to die an accursed death on the cross. It was in order to atone, as an innocent, for the guilty, in other words to bring about forgiveness of their sins. The assurance of forgiveness of personal guilt through the death of Jesus underlies the earlier 'surrender formula', as it does the creed of the dying of the Messiah for us.

How were the disciples able to justify this new assurance of forgiveness after Easter, beginning with the first eyewitness, Simon Peter, who denied his master, through James, who untrustingly had opposed his physical brother (cf. John 7.5), to the last of them all, Saul – Paul, who hated the Messiah and persecuted his followers? How did they know that the Son of Man had been given up *for them*? The stories of the appearances of Jesus, with their legendary elaborations, do not tell explicitly of a promise of forgiveness from the risen Lord, but they do mention the continual unbelief of the disciples and the way in which it was corrected (Matt. 28.17; Luke 24.11, 25, 38; John 20.19, 25, 29; 21.12, 16ff.). On the other hand, at least the emphatic greeting of 'Peace' from the risen Lord (Luke 24.36; John 20.19, 21, 26) is to be understood as a promise of salvation. We can hardly doubt that the question how the disciples could be sure that their secession and flight in Gethsemane (like Peter's denunciation) had been forgiven and settled must have been a decisive presupposition for their own missionary preaching about the eschatological reconciliation of sin by Christ. This can also be said about James, the formerly unbelieving brother of Jesus (John 7.5; cf. Mark 3.21 and The Gospel according to the Hebrews in Jerome, *De viris inlustribus* 2), and last but not least about the latest witness to the resurrection (I Cor. 15.8f.), Paul, the former persecutor and blasphemer of Christ (Gal. 1.13; Phil. 3.6; cf. I Cor. 15.9). The experience of forgiveness was surely of basic importance in his encounter with the risen Jesus before Damascus. This experience, that God in Jesus 'justifies the ungodly' (Rom. 4.5), made him from the very start the apostle to the Gentiles. This encounter with the risen Christ gave all witnesses the certainty that they were no longer 'still in their sins' (cf. I Cor. 15.11). As a result of the passion of Jesus, the question of guilt, which had already played a role in the preaching of John the Baptist and which was closely bound up with the conduct and the message of Jesus, was once again raised in a new and more radical fashion. In contrast to the preaching of John the Baptist, who connected forgiveness with the specific action of personal repentance and its consequences, this completely new certainty, produced by the appearances of the risen Jesus, was based on the act of the love of God through his Messiah, preceding all human action, in other words through the *extra nos* as Luther understood it, or, to use the earliest soteriological statement which we know, in the *service of the Son of Man* who gave his life as 'the ransom for many', that is, for everyone. At the same time this provides an answer to the burning question: why did the Messiah have to suffer? This assurance of forgiveness was hardly the result of a lengthy development bound up with theoretical scribal reflection, preceded by a primarily 'non-soteriological' interpretation of the death of Jesus and his resurrection; rather, as is shown by the old surrender formula which is quoted by Paul in Rom. 4.25, the death of the Messiah and his resurrection or exaltation from the dead was understood, in terms of the salvation thus given, as an indissoluble unity:

> Who was surrendered for our trespasses,
> and raised for our justification.

As a result, it is wrong to regard the two-membered credal formulae which confess the unity of Jesus' dying for us and his resurrection as secondary in theological content to the one-membered statements, say about the raising of Jesus by God. There is no clear way of pointing to a pure resurrection kerygma without a soteriological interpretation of the death of Jesus. Conversely, it was also impossible to refer only to the death of Jesus, without confessing his resurrection: 'If Christ has not been raised, your faith is futile and you are still in your sins' (I Cor. 15.17). The content of this statement of Paul's essentially applied from the beginning: through the resurrection the death of the Messiah Jesus was manifested as valid and effective representative atonement by God himself.

If in this way the kerygma of the death and resurrection of Jesus for our salvation prove to be a unity which cannot be separated in terms of content, or chronologically, even at the time of the origin of the church, a last question nevertheless remains. How did it come about that the disciples, essentially against the predominant contemporary messianic tradition now known to us, on the basis of

their encounter with the risen Jesus, came to understand the
crucifixion of Jesus as an eschatological saving event in the sense
of the universal vicarious atoning death of the Messiah?

If the roots of this lay *only* in scribal messianic interpretation of
Isaiah 53, it would have to be possible to demonstrate something
like a lengthy process of development within the soteriological
interpretation of the death of Jesus. However, this is improbable,
as an independent unsoteriological interpretation of the death of
Jesus and his resurrection cannot be shown to be the earliest
tradition. Reference should not be made in this context to the
hymn in Philippians or Peter's speeches in Acts, because a
soteriological understanding of the death of Jesus is taken for
granted in these relatively late texts.

It is also striking that the early kerygmatic formulae very soon
qualify the universal 'for all' and reduce it to 'for us', meaning the
community of believers. This is clear, for example, from a comparison of Mark 10.45 and I Tim. 2.6 with other surrender
formulae or of Mark 14.24 with I Cor. 11.24 (cf. however, 10.17).
This understandable tendency to reduce the scope of salvation to
one's own community presumably already began with the events of
Easter, which only affected a limited group.

Methodologically, then, we are justified, indeed compelled, to
push our enquiry *back to Jesus himself.* He was certainly anything
but an other-worldly fanatic, who unsuspectingly went to meet his
death in Jerusalem. It should no longer be doubted that he reckoned
with the possibility of his own execution, at the latest after that of
John the Baptist. What later community could have had any
interest in subsequently constructing such an obscure, indeed
questionable saying as Luke 12.50? The Gethsemane story was
also a constant cause of mockery and scorn for the anti-Christian
polemicists of antiquity.[61] The temptation of Jesus in the garden
completely went against any ancient ideal of martyrdom. It is more
difficult to answer the question how he understood and interpreted
his way to death. Within the framework of his proclamation of the
dawn of the kingdom of God he must also have considered the
increasingly threatening possibility of a violent death. Indeed he
was one of those gifted men who are in a position to see through

situations and people. Even the most radical sceptic cannot avoid
the simple historical question how this simple wandering teacher
and his outwardly inglorious death exercised such a tremendous and
unique influence that it still remains unsurpassed.[62] Some of the
reasons for this must lie *in the person and actions of Jesus* himself,
not least in the face of the threat of his death. Here the question is
concentrated above all on Jesus' last struggle in Jerusalem. Here
too we again come up against the unique agreement of our earliest
written evidence, Paul and Mark, in their accounts of the Last
Supper.

As Joachim Jeremias has made the essential points in this
particularly controversial area,[63] and Rudolf Pesch has largely
confirmed his arguments, I need only give a brief summary. On
the night before his death, 'in which he was betrayed' (or 'delivered
up': I Cor. 11.23), Jesus celebrated the passover meal with his
disciples and in it – presumably in parallel to the traditional words
of interpretation which explained what was happening at the meal
– in a symbolic action he related the broken bread to the breaking
of his body and at the end of the meal the wine in the cup of
blessing to the pouring out of his blood, through which the new
eschatological covenant with God would be founded and atonement would be achieved for all. In this way, at the same time he
represented his imminent death as the eschatological saving event
which – in connection with Isa. 53 – in the context of the dawn of
the kingdom of God brought about reconciliation with God for all
Israel, indeed for all men, and sealed God's eschatological new
covenant with his creatures. We are probably to understand Mark
14.25, the reference to the coming meal in the kingdom of God, as
meaning that Jesus wanted to prepare the way for the coming of
the kingdom of God through his sacrificial death in the face of the
apparent supremacy of evil and sin in God's own people and all
mankind. Of course we can only put all this forward as a hypothesis,
justified though it may be. Here we come up against the ultimate
mystery of Jesus' career.

Their encounter with the risen Lord confirmed for the disciples
this legacy of Jesus, the meaning of which had been overshadowed
by the catastrophe of the sudden arrest and shameful crucifixion of

Jesus and their own failure, which immediately followed. It was not primarily their own theological reflections, but above all the interpretative sayings of Jesus at the Last Supper which showed them how to understand his death properly. As a saying of Jesus, Mark 10.45 probably also belongs in the context of that last night; it will have been used by him to elucidate his mysterious symbolic action. From Luke (22.24) and Mark (13.12) we hear independently of each other that Jesus spoke at the Last Supper about 'serving'. He will hardly have done this without including his imminent fate. The saying over the cup and the saying about ransom are connected by the universal service 'for the many', in the sense of 'for all', which is presumably to be derived from Isaiah 53. This boundlessness of the appropriation of salvation matches the freedom of the proclamation and the activity of Jesus towards all the outcast, the lost and the sinners in Israel.

As it took place at least weekly, the celebration of the eucharist after Easter could no longer bear the features of the yearly passover meal; it was probably originally understood as a Todah sacrificial meal of the risen Lord.[64] Here people thought both of his vicarious sacrifice of his life on the cross and his exaltation and hoped-for coming again. The words with which Jesus interpreted the last supper with his disciples came to occupy a central place, because in it Jesus had dedicated to the disciples, his people – and beyond them to all men – the fruits of his violent death. The saving significance of his representative dying was probably expressed primarily at the common meal, in constantly new ways – on the basis of Jesus' own words. At each Lord's Supper, the first Christians proclaimed 'the Lord's death until he comes' (I Cor. 11.26). For that reason, this meal, along with the promise of the forgiveness of sins, came to lie at the heart of early Christian liturgy.

We now return to the question which was raised at the beginning. From a formal point of view, there are a whole series of analogies between Graeco-Roman, and even more Jewish, conceptions of atonement and the primitive Christian interpretation of the death of Jesus as representative atonement. However, seen in total, the event described in the New Testament breaks through the ancient conceptual framework and even goes beyond contemporary Jewish parallels. It concerns not only the unheard-of scandal that here the Son of God died on the cross the most shameful death known to the Roman world, but also the universality of the atonement brought about by this Son, involving all men, which not only warded off the anger of a God at particular misdeeds, but blotted out all human guilt and thus – as an eschatological act in the perspective of the dawning kingdom of God – reconciled the apostate creatures with their Creator.

It was consistent with this, and indeed necessary, that the pre-Pauline Greek-speaking community should have interpreted the death of the Messiah on the cross as an event which, more than the death of a pure martyr and righteous sufferer, stemmed from God himself and therefore at the same time recognized the crucified one as the pre-existent Son of God and mediator at creation, whom the Father had sent into the world to redeem his creation (Rom. 8.3; Gal. 4.4; Phil. 2.6–11; I Cor. 8.6; Col. 1.15ff.).[65] In the last resort, in the man Jesus of Nazareth God took death upon himself (cf. II Cor. 5.18ff; John 1.1, 14; 19.30). This did not in any way diminish the 'scandal of the cross'; indeed it *accentuated it, to an unprecedented degree for the ancient world.* But that means that in essentials we can only talk about the saving significance of the death of Jesus in appropriate theological terms if we talk of him in a 'trinitarian context'. Of course this basic theological problem, which we should never lose sight of, far transcends the framework of this study, which has been deliberately restricted to the historical developments between Jesus and Paul and their religious and historical background. For Paul and John – and not only for them – the voluntary self-sacrifice of the sinless Son of God which took place once and for all was the unsurpassable expression of God's free love:

But God shows his love for us in that while we were yet sinners Christ died for us (Rom. 5.8).

In this is love, not that we loved God but that he loved us and sent his Son to be the expiation for our sins (I John 4.10).

Here we are concerned not simply with a mythical view which has now become obsolete and which could be put aside without further ado; here – we may confidently affirm – perhaps in a mythical form which at first seems strange to us,[66] we come up against the heart of the gospel which grounds and supports our faith as it did of the first witnesses. It is the prime task of theology to show what lies at this heart in the language of our own time.

NOTES

Chapter One

1. M. Hengel, *Die Zeloten*, AGAJU 1, ²1976, 265f., 333, 353ff. and index 475 s.v. 'Kreuzigung'.

2. The dissertation by M.-L. Gubler, *Die frühesten Deutungen des Todes Jesu*, OBO 15, Freiburg 1977, gives an instructive account of most recent attempts at interpretation. Of course, at the same time it also shows the limitations of modern exegesis. As it discusses all recent publications, I need not give an extensive bibliography here.

3. I have tried to do some demolition work on this false alternative in *Judaism and Hellenism, Studies in their Encounter in Palestine in the Early Hellenistic Period*, London and Philadelphia 1974. Cf. *Jews, Greeks and Barbarians*, London and Philadelphia 1980. For Galilean Jewry cf. Seán Freyne, *Galilee from Alexander the Great to Hadrian, 320 BC to 153 CE*, Notre Dame 1980.

4. Klaus Wengst, *Christologische Formeln und Lieder des Urchristentums*, StNT 7, Gütersloh 1972, 70: 'The conception of the representative atoning death was developed in Hellenistic rather than Palestinian Judaism.' It was 'Hellenistic Judaism which stressed the notion of the representative atoning death, which was not current in Palestinian Judaism before Christianity and in the early Christian period. This suggests that we should also assume that the interpretation of the death of Jesus originated in the Christianity which came out of Hellenistic Judaism, i.e. in Hellenistic Jewish Christianity.' Cf. also M.-L. Gubler, op. cit., 252ff.

5. Gubler, op. cit., 34ff., 95ff., 200ff. The main treatment in a monograph of the theme of the suffering righteous man, which is so popular today, can be found in L. Ruppert, *Der leidende Gerechte*, Würzburg 1972; *Jesus als der leidende Gerechte*, SBS 59, Stuttgart 1972.

6. Apollodorus 2,7,7. Cf. the development of the hero's voluntary death in Seneca, *Hercules Oetaeus*. F. Pfister, *ARW* 34, 1937, even conjectured that a 'primal gospel' underlying all four gospels has been influenced by a 'Stoic-Cynic biography of Heracles' (59). H. J. Rose, *HTR* 31, 1938, 113–42, rightly attacked this. Among other features, Pfister (53) referred to Jesus' death-cry *tetelestai* in John 19.30 and the

threefold *peractum est* of *Herc. Oet.* 1340, 1457, 1472. However, there it is simply a matter of the hero suffering his fate: *fata se nostra explicant* (1472). On the other hand, see Rose's parallels between the ascension of Heracles and the two Lucan ascension accounts: 'There is a certain resemblance between the accounts of the two ascensions' (124). On this point see also Marcel Simon, *Hercule et le christianisme*, Paris 1955, and M. Mühl, 'Des Herakles Himmelfahrt', *RhMus* 101, 1958, 106–34. In general on the ancient ascension and transportation stories see N. Lohfink, *Die Himmelfahrt Jesu*, SANT 26, Munich 1971, 32ff.

7. *Iliad* 18,114ff., cf. 9,410ff.; in this connection Plato, *Symposium* 179d–180b makes Achilles an example of ὑπεραποθνῄσκειν or ἐπαποθνῄσκειν motivated by love, and compares him with Alcestis. For the apotheosis cf. H. Hommel, *Der Gott Achilleus*, SAH 1980, 1.

8. For his task see *Apology* 29a–31c, cf. 30a: 'For the god commands this' (ταῦτα γὰρ κελεύει ὁ θεός). For his death see *Crito*, especially the last remark, 54d: 'Well, then, Crito, let us act in this way, since it is in this way that the god leads us' (ἐπειδὴ ταύτῃ ὁ θεὸς ὑφηγεῖται); *Phaedo* 115b–118a, esp. 117b/c, his prayer to the gods before drinking the fatal draught, 'that my departure hence be a fortunate one'.

9. See the article by K. v. Fritz, 'Peregrinus (Proteus)', *PW* 19, 1, 1937, cols. 656–63.

10. N. Lohfink, op. cit., gives the best summary, 32–50.

11. L. Wächter, *Der Tod im Alten Testament*, AzTh II, 8, Stuttgart 1967; H. Gese, *Zur biblischen Theologie*, BEvTh 78, Munich 1977, 31–54: 'The Old Testament is familiar with such traditions (of heroes), but its concern for God does not allow a cult of heroes any more than it allows idolatry' (35).

12. On this see U. Kellermann, *Auferstanden in den Himmel. 2 Makkabäer 7 und die Auferstehung der Märtyrer*, SBS 95, Stuttgart 1979; following H. v. Campenhausen, *Die Idee des Martyriums in der Alten Kirche*, Göttingen ²1964, 153f., he refers to the example of the martyr philosopher (46ff.). The most recent work, T. Baumeister, *Die Anfänge der Theologie des Martyriums*, Munster 1980, pays too little attention to the Greek roots of the ideology of martyrdom. But cf. his concession on pp. 12f.: apart from Isa. 53, Israel did not have any 'theology of martyrdom' even in connection with the murder of prophets.

13. The few texts which are to some extent an exception here mostly go back to the archaic period. The Song of Deborah (Judg. 5.18) praises Zebulon as 'a people which despised its life, prepared for death' ('*am ḥerep napšō lāmūt*), and Judg. 9.17 says that Jerubbaal-Gideon 'fought for you (= Israel), hazarded his life (*wayyašlek napšō*, i.e. put his life at stake) and delivered you from the hand of Midian'. This mode of expression is quite extraordinary; its closest parallel is in Isa. 53.12:

he 'eᵉra lammawet napšō, cf. also n.19 below. We also find the formula *šīm* (*'et*) *napšō bᵉkappō*, I Sam. 19.5, cf. 28.21; Judg. 12.3; Job 13.14: take his life in his hands, risk the utmost.

14. Both Zech. 14.10ff. and 13.7ff., the saying about the death of the shepherd, could have a concealed reference to the death of a messianic figure. However, the saving significance of this figure remains cryptic, and can only be inferred indirectly from 14.10a; 13.1f. and 13.9b. On this see W. Rudolph, *Haggai-Sacharja 1–8—Sacharja 9–14—Maleachi*, KAT XII, 4, Gütersloh 1976, 211ff., who conjectures a connection with the servant of God in Isa. 53 (213f., 223f.). The text already belongs in the Hellenistic period (163, 211): the *terminus a quo* is *c*.350, the *terminus ad quem* 200. Cf. also H. Gese (op. cit., n.11), 137: 'Although . . . this figure does not appear as a bringer of salvation, but as one who has fallen in the battles of the end-time, he leads his people along the way to the new covenant.' In 12.10ff. there is also an indirect reference to the conception of the resurrection, as there is in Isa. 26.19ff., which comes from about the same time (52).

15. For details see O. H. Steck, *Israel und das gewaltsame Geschick der Propheten*, WMANT 23, Neukirchen-Vluyn 1967; of course he puts rather too much emphasis on the traditio-historical significance of the theme. Cf. M.-L. Gubler, op. cit., 34–94; T. Baumeister, op. cit., 6–13.

16. *EvTh* 26, 1966, 237.

17. Deut. 24.16. The text is quoted in two other places: II Kings 14.6; II Chron. 25.4. On this see K. Wengst, op. cit., 65f.

18. Ex. 32.30–33, cf. H. Gese, op. cit., 88: 'Moses wants to make atonement, offers himself as *kōper*, i.e. offers his existence which is written in the book of life. This is a substitute offering of his life through a total representative sacrifice.'

19. I Macc. 2.50: ζηλώσατε τῷ νόμῳ καὶ δότε τὰς ψυχὰς ὑμῶν ὑπὲρ διαθήκης πατέρων ἡμῶν. Cf. T. Baumeister, op. cit., (n.12), 138f. For the formula cf. Dan. 3.28 (see above, p. 12) and the later rabbinic terminology.

20. *Antt.* 12.281: ὥστε ἀποθανεῖν ὑπὲρ τῶν νόμων, ἂν δέη, cf. 267,282; cf. Aristotle, *Nicomachaean Ethics* 1169a, 18ff.: ἀληθὲς δὲ περὶ τοῦ σπουδαίου καὶ τὸ τῶν φίλων ἕνεκα πολλὰ πράττειν καὶ τῆς πατρίδος, κἂν δέη ὑπεραποθνήσκειν. Cf. Epictetus, *Diss.* 2.7.3.

21. Dying for freedom: Josephus, *BJ* 3. 357; cf. *Antt.* 12.433; 13.5; for the Jewish people, *Antt.* 13.1; 6; for the Law: *BJ* 1.650; 2.6; *Antt.* 15.288; *Contra Apionem* 1.42f.; II Macc. 7.19; 8.21: ἑτοίμους ὑπὲρ τῶν νόμων καὶ τῆς πατρίδος ἀποθνήσκειν, III Macc. 1.23; IV Macc. 6.27: διὰ τὸν νόμον; 9.1; 13.9; περὶ τοῦ νόμου; Philo, *Leg.* 215: καὶ προαποθνήσκειν αἱρουμένους τῶν πατρίων. Cf. also *Ass. Mos.* 9.6: *et moriamur potius, quam praetereamus mandata domini dominorum* . . . cf.

M. Hengel, op. cit. (n.1); U. Kellermann, op. cit. (n.12), 20; and K. Wengst, op. cit. (n.4), 68f.; T. Baumeister, op. cit., 39–62.

22. I Macc. 6.44: ἔδωκεν ἑαυτὸν τοῦ σῶσαι τὸν λαὸν αὐτοῦ καὶ περιποιῆσαι ἑαυτῷ ὄνομα αἰώνιον. For the theme of glory among the Greeks see G. Steinkopf, *Untersuchungen zur Geschichte des Ruhmes bei den Griechen*, Diss. phil. Halle-Wittenberg 1937 (up to Thucydides). For Judaism see the praise of the fathers in Sir. 44.1; 46.2; 47.6; 49.13; 50.1. K. Wengst, op. cit. (n.4), 68 n.S8, makes the wild guess that in two texts from I Maccabees, originally written in Hebrew, 2.50f. and 6.44, 'the assumption of a Jewish-Hellenistic interpolation is inescapable', since 'these statements . . . are so isolated in the Palestinian Jewish sphere and are so little different from Greek and Hellenistic Jewish parallels'. However, this distinction in principle is extremely questionable.

23. Euripides, *Alcestis* 18, 178, 282ff., 339ff., 383, 434, 472, 524, 620, 644f., 649, 682, 684, 690, 698, 701, 710, 716, 1002f. The prepositions which express representativeness change: in addition to ὑπέρ we also find πρό and ἀντί. For Alcestis cf. also Apollodorus, *Library*, 1.9.5.

24. 968f.: αὐτός . . .
θνῄσκειν ἕτοιμος πατρίδος ἐκλυτήριον.

25. 997f. (cf. 1056, 1090: Κρέοντος παῖς ὁ γῆς ὑπερθανών).). The emphatic 'I go' may be an allusion to the resolve of Achilles (see n. 7 above).

26. *Heraclides*, 550f.: . . . τὴν ἐμὴν ψυχὴν ἐγὼ
δίδωμ' ἑκοῦσα τοῖσδ', ἀναγκασθεῖσα δ'οὔ,
cf. 501f., 509f., 530ff.: 'For this life (ψυχή) is ready, willing and ungrudging. And I proclaim that I die for my brothers and for myself. Not loving my life (μὴ φιλοψυχοῦσ' ἐγώ), I made this supreme discovery: gloriously to leave it.' For the stress on free will cf. John 10.18.

27. Cf. *Symposium* 208d (and 207b). Other examples given by Plato in addition to Alcestis are Achilles and the Athenian king Codrus (see p. 22 above). The theme of love is not of itself enough for vicarious death: it must be supplemented by the 'immortal remembrance of their *aretē*' and the hope of a 'noble reputation, for they love the immortal'. This theme appears in the New Testament in Rom. 5.6–8 and John 15.13.

28. *Iliad* 15.495–8, cf. 24.500 and 12.243, which according to Diodore 15.52.4 was quoted by Epaminondas before the battle of Leuctra (again a quotation from Hector): εἷς οἰωνὸς ἄριστος ἀμύνεσθαι περὶ πάτρης, 'One thing is the best sign, to fight for one's country.' Tyrtaeus no. 6, ed. C. Prato, Rome 1968, 27. There are further parallels there, see H. Hommel, 'Dulce et Decorum . . .', *RhMus* 111, 1968, 219–52 (236ff.). For Callinus see fr. 1.6f., ed. J. M. Edmonds, *Elegy and Iambus*, LCL 1.44.

29. Strabo 9.4.2 (425 C) = W. Peek, *Griechische Grabgedichte*, Darmstadt 1960, no. 3. Cf. also no. 9.3; 14.2; 17.4; 21.5; 32; and the private epitaphs no. 125.1; 130.3; 136.5; 173.5; 457.11f. See further on the shared death of the father and his seven-year-old son, 272.5f.: ἀντὶ χοῶν δ'ὁ πατὴρ ψυχὴν ἰδίαν ἐπέδωκεν κοινὸν ἔχειν ἐθέλων οὔνομα καὶ θάνατον, 'instead of a libation the father gave his own life. He did not want (only) to share a name (with you) but also death.' The chief prepositions are περί, ὑπέρ and πρό.

30. 237a: τὴν τελευτὴν ἀντὶ τῆς τῶν ζώντων σωτηρίας ἠλλάξαντο, cf. 243a, 246b.

31. Fragment 66, O. Werner (78, B. Snell et al.), see LCL, p. 556; Plutarch, *De Gloria Atheniensium* 7 (349c), attributes this verse to Epaminondas when he and the Thebans 'sacrificed themselves in the finest and most glorious battles for their country, its tombs and sanctuaries' (ὑπὲρ πατρίδος καὶ τάφων καὶ ἱερῶν ἐπιδιδόντες ἑαυτοὺς τοῖς καλλίστοις καὶ λαμπροτάτοις ἀγῶσιν). Athenagoras, *Apology* 19a, ascribes the verse to Pindar and stresses that it is inspired by the heroic spirit of the *Iliad*. For the sacrificial terminology cf also Euripides, *Erechtheus* fr. 79.38f.: κόρην/θῦσαι πρὸ γαίας; Plutarch, *Pelopidas* 21.2: Λεωνίδαν τε τῷ χρησμῷ τρόπον τινὰ προθυσάμενον ἑαυτὸν ὑπὲρ τῆς Ἑλλάδος.

32. 'Martyriumsparänese und Sühnetod in synoptischen und jüdischen Traditionen', in *Die Kirche des Anfangs. Festschrift für Heinz Schürmann*, Leipzig 1977, 223–46 (238).

33. Aristides 21, cf. Diodore 11.33.3 and the account by W. Burkert, *Homo necans*, 1972, 68f. For the cult of heroes and sacrifice to the dead see L. R. Farnell, *Greek Hero Cults and Ideas of Immortality*, 1921, and W. Burkert, *Griechische Religion der archäischen und klassischen Epoche*, 1977, 293ff., 313ff.

34. Fr. 5 Diels: εὐκλεὴς μὲν ἁ τύχα, καλὸς δ'ὁ πότμος, βωμὸς δ'ὁ τάφος, πρὸ χόων δὲ μνᾶστις, ὁ δ'οἶνος ἔπαινος. ἐντάφιον δὲ τοιοῦτον εὐρὼς οὔθ'ὁ πανταδαμάτωρ ἀμαυρώσει χρόνος ἀνδρῶν ἀγαθῶν, ὁ δὲ σηκὸς οἰκέταν εὐδοξίαν Ἑλλάδος εἵλετο. See H. Fränkel, *Dichtung und Philosophie des frühen Griechentums*, ³1969, 365, cf. 366: 'Thus the fallen are declared to be effective heroes, like the great dead of mythical times, whose tombs are at the same time also sanctuaries'.

35. Cf. M. Hengel, *Jews, Greeks and Barbarians*, London and Philadelphia 1980, 55ff.

36. L. R. Farnell (n. 33), 362: 'The cult is a reward for patriotism, for a noble death against the national foe.' 363: 'Such honours for great public services may well have had a certain social value as a stimulus to effort and sacrifice; for their appeal to the vanity of the Hellene, whatever was his actual faith in these matters, must have been strongly felt.'

37. Plutarch, *Apophthegmata Lacedaimonia* (*Leonidas Ano.* 10) 225C. Cf. (no. 4) 225A; cf. the quotation from *Pelopidas* 21.2, and n. 31 above. Further Isocrates 4 (*Panegyric*) 90–92; 6 (*Archidamus*) 100; Lysias, *Epitaphios* 26; Lycurgus, *Oratio in Leocratem* 24 (104); 28 (109), etc.; Polybius 9.38.4: μὴ μόνον ⟨ὑπὲρ⟩ τῆς αὐτῶν, ἀλλὰ καὶ περὶ τῆς τῶν ἄλλων Ἑλλήνων ἐλευθερίας προκινδυνεύειν.

38. 2.43.1/2 . . . κάλλιστον δὲ ἔρανον αὐτῇ (sc. τῇ πόλει) προϊέμενοι. κοινῇ γὰρ τὰ σώματα διδόντες ἰδίᾳ τὸν ἀγήρων ἔπαινον ἐλάμβανον, cf. Isocrates 4 (*Panegyric*) 75: τοὺς τοῖς σώμασιν ὑπὲρ τῆς Ἑλλάδος προκινδυνεύσαντας. For the terminology cf. W. Popkes, *Christus Traditus*, 1967, 86f. Libanius, *Declamationes* 24.23 (ed. Foerster 6.458, line 5) which he quotes: ἀναμνήσθητε τῶν ἐν Πύλαις ὑπὲρ ἐλευθερίας τῶν Ἑλλήνων δεδωκότων τὰ σώματα is dependent on the earlier terminology of Thucydides and Isocrates.

39. *wihabū gešmᵉhōn di lā' yiplᵉḥūn* . . . LXX καὶ παρέδωκαν τὰ σώματα αὐτῶν εἰς ἐμπυρισμόν, ἵνα μὴ λατρεύσωσι . . . cf. I Cor. 13.3.

40. 4 (*Panegyric*) 77; cf. 75 (n. 38 above). The formula appears particularly frequently in the 'pan-Hellenic' Isocrates. Cf. also 4.62, 83, 95, 154; 5 (*Philip*). 55, 135: ὑπὲρ δὲ τοῦ τυχεῖν καλῆς δόξης ἀποθνῄσκειν ἐν τοῖς πολέμοις ἐθέλοντας; 6 (*Archidamus*). 93f., 107; 12 (*Panathenaicus*), 185: κινδυνεύειν ὑπὲρ τῆς πατρίδος, 186: περὶ τῶν ἀλλοτρίων ἑτοίμως ἀποθνῄσκειν; 20 (*Lochites*), 20: ἀποθνῄσκειν ὑπὲρ τῆς πολιτείας.

41. Lysias 2 (*Epitaphios*). 68; Demosthenes, 18 (*De corona*) 205: 20 (*contra Lept.*) 83; 26 (*contra Aristogeiton II*). 23; Lycurgus, *Oratio in Leocratem* 27 (104) and often.

42. Polybius 2.30.4; Gauls: καὶ διδόντες σφᾶς αὐτοὺς ἑκουσίως ἀπέθνῃσκον; 9.38.4; 15,10,3; 16,34,11; Dio Chrysostom 32, 48f.; Plutarch, *Moralia* 219B; 238A; *Brutus* 40, and often.

43. *Topica* 22, 84: see also below p. 82, n. 49.

44. POx Col. I = Acta Alexandrinorum XI B lines 11ff. On this see the commentary by H. A. Musurillo, *The Acts of the Pagan Martyrs*, 1954, 215, 237.

45. For Aristotle see above p. 78 n. 20. E. Schwartz, *Ethik der Griechen*, 1951, 121. For the εὔλογος ἐξαγωγή of the Stoa see von Arnim, *SVF* III, fr. 757 = Diogenes Laertius 7,130 and fr. 768, the anonymous *Excerpta philosophica*, Cod. Coislin 387, and on this E. Benz, *Das Todesproblem in der stoischen Philosophie*, 1929, 69ff. Epicurus: see H. Usener, *Epicurea* no. 590 = Diogenes Laertius 10.121, cf. on this E. Schwartz, op. cit., 191, and A. Deissmann, *Light from the Ancient East*, London ²1927, 118 n. 1, the quotation from the biography of the Epicurean Philonides and Rom. 16.4. For Epictetus see *Diss*, 2.7.3: 'To incur danger for a friend when necessary, indeed even to die for him'.

For the philosophical tradition see the commentary by R. A. Gauthier and J. Y. Jolif, *Aristote, L'Ethique à Nicomaque* II, 1959, 748ff.

46. Cf. A. Oltramare, *Les Origines de la diatribe romaine*, Thèse Gèneve 1926, 52f., 60f., 285f. See also index s.v. 'guerre', 'état', 'mort'. A later example, of an undeterred philosophical 'martyr', also cited relatively often in the Jewish and Christian tradition, was the Cynic Anaxarchos from the time of Alexander. See Diels-Kranz, *Vorsokratiker*, no. 72; Diogenes Laertius 9.59f.; Philo, *Quod omnis* 106–9; Clement of Alexandria, *Stromateis* 4.57. Cf. A. Alföldi, 'Der Philosoph als Zeuge der Wahrheit . . .' *Scientiis Artibusque. Collectanea Academiae Hungaricae* I, Rome 1958, 7–19 (8).

47. *Odes* 3.2.13, cf. H. Hommel, 'Dulce et decorum . . .' *RhMus* 111, 1968, 219–52, also *Odes* 3.12.2 and 4.9.50ff. (the description of the *recte beatus*):

> Peiusque leto flagitium timet,
> Non ille pro caris amicis
> aut patria timidus perire.

'He is afraid of evil more than of death; he is not afraid to die for dear friends or for his homeland.' For the difficult *dulce* cf. H. Usener (n. 45), 338f., 601, esp. Seneca, *Ep.* 66.18; and Pausanias 9,17,1 on Antipoinos and his two daughters: Ἀντιποίνῳ μὲν οὖν. . . οὐχ ἡδὺ ἦν ἀποθνήσκειν πρὸ τοῦ δήμου, ταῖς δὲ Ἀντιποίνου θυγατράσιν ἤρεσκε. ('Antipoinos did not find it sweet to die for the people, but it pleased his two daughters.')

48. Cf. Scherling, *PW* 11, 1, cols. 984ff. See Hellanikos, FGrHist 4 fr. 125: ὃς καὶ ὑπὲρ τῆς πατρίδος ἀπέθανε, or Horace 3.19.2: *Codrus pro patria non timidus mori.* The earliest extant account of the saga appears in Lycurgus, *Oratio in Leocratem* 20 (84–89): τοὺς πολεμίους ἐξαπατῶντες ἀποθνήσκειν ὑπὲρ αὐτῆς (sc. τῆς πατρίδος).

49. Cicero, *Tusculan Disputations* 1.48f., 116f.; cf. 1.37,89. On this cf. H. W. Litchfield, 'National *Exempla virtutis* in Roman Literature', *Harvard Studies in Classical Literature* 25, 1914, 1–73. For Vercingetorix see Caesar, *De bello gallico* 7.89: *et quoniam sit fortunae cedendum, ad utramque rem seillis offerre, seu morte sua Romanis satisfacere seu vivum tradere velint.*

50. Dio Cassius, *Epitome* 63.13f. For the suicides of soldiers at his death see Tacitus, *Histories* 2.49.4; *non noxa neque ob metum, sed aemulatione decoris et caritate principis.*

51. I Clement 55. 1–5.

52. Virgil, *Aeneid* 5.815. Cf. in Plutarch, *Phocion* 17.3, the reply of the politician to his enemies confronted with the demands of Alexander the Great: τὸ μὲν γὰρ αὐτὸς ὑπὲρ ὑμῶν ἁπάντων ἀποθανεῖν εὐτυχίαν ἂν ἐμαυτοῦ θείμην. Libanius, *Declaratio* 42, 46 (Foerster 7,415). For the Roman *Devotio* see Livy 5.41.2: *eos se pro patria Quiritibusque*

Romanis tradant. Cf. F. Schwenn, *Die Menschenopfer bei den Griechen und Römern*, 1915, 154ff.; Patsch, *PW* 5.1, cols. 277ff., K. Latte, *Römische Religionsgeschichte*, ²1967, see index s.v., see also p. 23 and n. 90. 53. Billerbeck 2.545f. (GenR 94,9): the advice given by R. Yehoshua b.Levi to hand over someone sought by the Roman authorities. The whole passage is in the context of the discussion of the handing over to Joab of Sheba son of Bichri: II Sam. 20.16ff., and that of Jeconiah to Nebuchadnezzar: II Kings 24.12. In Josephus, *De Bello Judaico* 6.95,103ff., Titus and Josephus asked for the leaders of the rebels to give themselves up to save the city, referring to the example of Jeconiah: αἰχμαλωσίαν ὑπέμεινεν ἐθελούσιον ὑπὲρ τοῦ μὴ παραδοῦναι ταῦτα πολεμίοις τὰ ἅγια καὶ τὸν οἶκον τοῦ θεοῦ περιιδεῖν φλεγόμενον.

54. Origen, *Contra Celsum* 2.45: οὔτε συναπέθανον οὔτε ὑπεραπέθανον αὐτοῦ.

55. Fr. 44, Diels/Kranz: I owe this reference to my colleague Eberhard Jüngel; Fr. 114; cf. also Fr. 24: 'Gods and men honour those who fall in war.' Heraclitus presupposes the high estimation of those fallen in war common among the Greeks of his time.

56. 26 (*Contra Aristogeiton* II), 23.

57. Cf. H. v. Campenhausen, *Die Idee des Martyriums in der alten Kirche*, ²1964, 153; 'The Christian martyr . . . . . . appears in the role of Socrates and explicitly refers to his example.' Cf. above pp. 4f.

58. Diogenes Laertius 5.7f. = Athenaeus 15, p. 696b–d (Aristotle, Fr. 674, 675 Rose). Cf. Theopompus, FGrHist 115 F 291, and I. Düring, 'Aristoteles', in *The Ancient Biographical Tradition*, 1957, 272ff.

59. Sirach 4.28. In Aramaic the root '*ṣ*' has the meaning 'press, oppress' and in Syriac *repugnare*, see C. Brockelmann, *Lexicon Syriacum*, 1928, 539b, with a reference to hebr. Sir.4.28.

60. Philostratus, *Vita Apollonii*, 7.12 beginning; 7.13 end; 7.14 beginning and end, ET, LCL 171–91. The closing quotation from *Iliad* 18.309 relates to a saying of Hector as he goes out to meet Achilles in battle.

61. Op. cit. (n. 4), 64. For the theme, cf. A. Alföldi, op. cit. (n. 46).

62. K. Fauth, *Der kleine Pauly* 4, 309. For the Hittites see H. M. Kümmel, 'Ersatzkönig und Sündenbock', *ZAW* 80, 1968, 289–318, cf. also W. Burkert, *Structure*, 59ff.; for the sacrifice of children throughout the Semitic world see O. Kaiser, 'Den Erstgeborenen deiner Söhne sollst du mir geben', *Denkender Glaube. Festschrift C. H. Ratschow, zum 65*, Berlin 1976, 24–48 (29ff.); and on this Philo Byblius in Eusebius, *Dmonstratio Evangelica* 4, 16, 11 (FGr-Hist 790, 3b): ἀντὶ τῆς πάντων φθορᾶς τὸ ἠγαπημένον τῶν τεκνῶν τοὺς κρατοῦντας ἢ πόλεως ἢ ἔθνους εἰς σφαγὴν ἐπιδιδόναι λύτρον τοῖς τιμωροῖς δαίμοσι. Philo Byblius supports

this with a reference to the Phoenician primal king Kronos-El, who sacrificed his firstborn in a time of extreme peril during a war.

63. In the first instance I would refer here to the basic investigations by W. Burkert, 'Greek Tragedy and Sacrificial Ritual', *Greek Roman and Byzantine Studies* 7, 1966, 87ff.,; *Homo necans*, 1972; *Griechische Religion der archaischen und klassischen Epoche*, 1977, 129ff., 139ff.; *Structure and History in Greek Mythology and Ritual*, 1979, 59ff., 168ff. I am grateful to him for sending me xeroxes of proofs of the last book and for some further references. Cf. also E. von Lasaulx, *Die Sühnopfer der Griechen und Römer und ihr Verhältnis zu dem einen auf Golgotha*, Würzburg 1841, and F. Schwenn, *Die Menschenopfer bei den Griechen und Römern*, 1915, still provide usable collections of material. The brief but full study by W. Speyer, 'Religionen des griechisch-römischen Bereichs. Zorn der Gottheit, Vergeltung und Sühne,' in *Theologie und Religionswissenschaft. Der gegenwärtige Stand ihrer Forschungsergebnisse*, ed. U. Mann, 1973, 124–43, is also instructive.

64. F. Schwenn (n. 63), 112ff., 119ff., and *PW* 15.1, cols. 948ff.; U. von Wilamowitz-Moellendorff, *Der Glaube der Hellenen*, ²1959, I, 293ff. For the repudiation see e.g. Porphyry, *De abstinentia* 2.54–56; in Plutarch see H. D. Betz (ed.), *Plutarch's Theological Writings and Early Christian Literature*, 1975. Index s.v. 'Sacrifice, human', 368. W. Burkert, *Homo necans*, index s.v. 'Menschenopfer', 348.

65. Burkert, op. cit., 56, with reference to Mommsen, *Römisches Strafrecht*, 1899, 900ff. According to Dionysus of Halicarnassus, *Antt.* 2.10.3, patrons and clients who broke contracts should be killed as traitors, in accordance with a law of Romulus, ὡς θῦμα τοῦ καταχθονίου Διός. Cf. Livy 3.55.7: *qui tribunis plebis, aedilibus . . . nocuisset, eius caput Iovi sacer est.* Cf. also C. Brecht, art. *'perduellio'*, *PW* 16.621f. Cf. M. Hengel, *Crucifixion*, 1977, 33ff., 86ff.

66. For Euripides, *Phoenissae* 911–1018, 1090ff., see above, p. 9. Cf. Höfer, *Roschers Lexikon* 2.2.2794f.; J. Schmitt, *Freiwilliger Opfertod bei Euripides*, 1921, index 105, s.v. *Phoenissae*, see espec. 12: 'Ares requires this human sacrifice as atonement for the slaughter of the earthborn dragon'; F. Schwenn, *Menschenopfer*, 134–7. It seems improbable that the sacrificial death of Menoeceus is an invention of Euripides. For the later influence of the sagas see Cicero, *Tusculans* 1. 48, 116. The description of Menoeceus' prayer of devotion to the gods in Statius, *Thebais* 10.768ff., is impressive:

> *at Tyriis* (i.e. the descendants of Cadmus in Thebes) *templa, arva, domos, conubia, natos*
> *reddite morte mea: si vos placita hostia iuvi,*
> *si non attonitis vatis consulta recepi*
> *auribus et Thebis nondum credentibus hausi*

haec Amphioniis pro me *persolvite tectis*
ac mihi deceptum, precor, exorate parentem.

As *devotus* he hurls himself down on the enemy from the walls and with his blood sprinkles and purifies the besieged city:
ast illum amplexae Pietas Virtusque ferebant,
leniter ad terras corpus; nam spiritus olim
ante Iovem et summis apicem sibi poscit in astris.
The expiatory sacrificial death is followed by the apotheosis of the hero. Hyginus, *Fabulae* 68: *Menoeceus cum vidit se unum civium salutem posse redimere, muro se praecipitavit.* Cf. also the anonymous figure in Ps. Quintilian, *Declamationes* 326 (Ritter, 282).

67. J. Schmitt (n. 66), see index s.v. and above all 13ff. In contrast to Aeschylus' *Agamemnon*, where 'Iphigenia is carried off to the altar as a defenceless sacrifice' and 'her cries and laments . . . did not touch her ambitious father', Euripides introduces the element of free will. For the various earlier versions of the sagas see H. von Geisau, *Der kleine Pauly*, 2.1447f.

68. Euripides, *Hecuba*, 343ff., 432ff., 518ff.; Seneca, *Troades* 193ff.; Ovid, *Metamorphoses* 13.448: *placet Achilleos mactata Polyxena manes.* J. Schmitt (n. 66), see index 105 s.v.

69. Lycurgus, *Oratio in Leocratem* 24 (98ff.) presents Erechtheus as a paradigm of a patriot and quotes a lengthy fragment from the lost play of Euripides: fr. 360 Nauck, = C. Austin, *Nova Fragmenta Euripidea*, 1968, 25ff.; there is also a collection of the various ancient accounts, 22ff. Cf. Aristides I, 19, Dindorf: τὴν θυγατέρα ὑπὲρ τῆς πόλεως ἐπιδοῦναι, τοῦ θεοῦ χρήσαντος, Apollodorus 3.15.4. The fragment Pap. Sorb 2328, Austin, op. cit., 33ff., contains the making of the three daughters into heroes by Athene: line 72: εἰς αἴθερ'αὐτῶν πνεῦμ' ἐγὼ [κ]ατώικισα, cf. also J. Schmitt (n. 66), 63ff. The daughter is often confused with her sisters, for whom a similar fate was prophesied (see p. 22 above). On this cf. Phanodemos, FGrHist 325F4 = Suidas, *Lexikon* s.v. παρθένοι: δοῦναι ἑαυτὰς σφαγῆναι ὑπὲρ τῆς χώρας.

70. M. P. Nilsson, *Geschichte der Griechischen Religion* 2, ²1965, 771: 'With Euripides the Enlightenment, with its particular discussion of problems, came on to the scene.' However, cf. E. R. Dodds, 'Euripides als Irrationalist', in *Der Fortschrittsgedanke in der Antike*, 1977, 97–112 (English version *The Ancient Concept of Progress*, 1973, 97–129).

71. J. Schmitt (n. 66), 1f., cf. P. Roussel, 'Le thème du sacrifice volontaire dans la tragédie d'Euripide', *Revue belge de philologie et d'histoire* 1, 1922, 225–40.

72. Cf. Schmitt (n. 66), 78. The group θύειν, θυσία, θῦμα only appears with frequency in the *Iphigenia*. Cf. also P. Stengel, *Opfer-bräuche der Griechen*, 1910, 92–104; W. Burkert, *Homo necans*, 16f. n. 42;

Greek Tragedy (n. 63), 102ff. Referring to R. K. Yerkes, *Sacrifice in Greek and Roman Religions and Early Judaism*, 1952, Burkert, op. cit., 103, stresses 'that Semitic (Phoenician and Hebrew) sacrificial rites offer the closest parallels to Greek ritual'.

73. J. Schmitt, op. cit., (n. 66), 11, 22ff., 39ff., 63ff.

74. Op. cit., (n. 71), 240, Cf. E. R. Dodds (n. 70), 108: 'What Euripides presents to us here is the incursion of the mystery behind life, of the "other which is dearer than life" (*Hippolytus* 191). Beside this other, the chorus sings, wisdom is the folly of the sophists (*Bacchae* 395).' Cf. René Girard, *La Violence et le Sacré*, 1972, 170ff.

75. Diogenes Laertius 1.110; Athenagoras 13.602c: Κρατῖνος ... ἑκὼν αὑτὸν ἐπέδωκεν ὑπὲρ τῆς θρεψαμένης· ᾧ καὶ ἐπαπέθανεν ὁ ἐραστὴς Ἀριστόδημος, λύσιν τ' ἔλαβε τὸ δεινόν, quoted from Neanthes of Cyzicus, *Peri teletōn* = FGrHist 84 F 16.

76. W. Burkert, *Structure and History* ... 72ff.; F. Schwenn (n. 63), 154ff.; S. Eitrem, 'Die göttlichen Zwillinge bei den Griechen', *Skrifter Videnskap Kristiania* II, 1903, no. 2, 72ff.

77. *Homo necans*, 76ff.; cf. *Structure*, 74ff.

78. Metioche and Menippe, Antonius Liberalis 25, ed. M. Papathomopulos, 1968, 43f., and commentary 125ff., Ovid, *Metamorphoses* 4,1,389ff.

79. Androcleia and Alcis, daughters of Antipoinos, Pausanias 9.17.1. Cf. F. Schwenn (n. 63), 128f.

80. Aelian, *Varia historia* 12.28: ταύτας δὲ ὑπὲρ τῆς πόλεως τῆς Ἀθηναίων ἀναιρεθῆναι λόγος ἔχει, ἐπιδόντος αὐτὰς τοῦ Λεὼ ἐς τὸν χρησμὸν τὸν Δελφιόν. ἔλεγε γὰρ μὴ ἂν ἄλλως σωθῆναι τὴν πόλιν, εἰ μὴ ἐκεῖναι σφαγιασθεῖεν. Cf. also Diodore 17.15.2, the speech of Phocion, opponent of Demosthenes, who, with reference to the example of the daughters of Leo and Hyacinthus, ὠνείδιζε τῶν μὴ βουλομένων ὑπὲρ τῆς πόλεως τελευτᾶν, see also pp. 12f., n. 52 They were partly confused with the daughters of Erechtheus, see Cicero, *De natura deorum* 3.50; so the tradition, too, is uncertain, although it is a question of a sacrifice or offering by the father, see the commentary by A. S. Pease on *De natura deorum*, ad loc., cf. also F. Schwenn (n. 63), 129f., and Kock, 'Leokorion', *PW* 12.2, cols. 2000f.

81. Apollodorus 3.15.8; Hyginus, *Fabulae* 238. They, too, are sometimes identified with the daughters of Erechtheus, as in Ps. Demosthenes 60.27; Suidas, *Lexicon*, s.v. παρθένοι, cf. F. Schwenn (n. 63), 131.

82. Philochorus, FGrHist 328F 105 + 106 (Schol. Dem. 19. 303): ... ἔχρησεν ὁ Ἀπόλλων ἀπαλλαγήσεσθαι ἐάν τις ἀνέλῃ ἑαυτὸν ὑπὲρ τῆς πόλεως· ἡ τοίνυν Ἄγραυλος ἑκοῦσα αὐτὴν ἐξέδωκεν εἰς θάνατον. ἔρριψε γὰρ ἑαυτὴν ἐκ τοῦ τείχους. εἶτα ἀπαλλαγέντος τοῦ πολέμου, ἱερὸν ὑπὲρ τούτου ἐστήσαντο αὐτῆι... For the oath of the ephebes see Plutarch,

Alcibiades 15.4. Cf. W. Burkert, *Homo necans*, 77f. For the complicated history of the tradition see F. Jacoby, FGrHist Supplement b, *A Commentary on the Ancient History of Athens*, I, 1954, 425ff., and II, 326ff.

83. Plutarch, *Theseus* 32.4: ἀφ'οὖ (=Marathos) δὲ Μαραθῶνα τὸν δῆμον, ἐπιδόντος ἑαυτὸν ἑκουσίως κατά τι λόγιον σφραγιάσασθαι πρὸ τῆς παρατάξεως. Cf. F. Schwenn (n. 52), 133.

84. J. Schmitt (n. 66), 83ff., who refers to Wilamowitz-Moellendorff; Roussel (n. 71) 229, n. 1 differs. The name, which already speaks for itself and indicates a heroizing, suggests a later formation. See also Wrede, *PW* 14.1, cols. 622f.

85. Cheiron: Apollodorus 2.5.4; 2.5.11: Χείρωνα ἀθάνατον ⟨ὄντα⟩ θνῆσκειν ἀντ'αὐτοῦ θέλοντα. For Augustus see Dio Cassius 80.20; Caligula: Suetonius, *Caligula* 27; Hadrian: *Historia Augusta* I (Spartian) 14; cf. also Suetonius, *Nero* 36; for the whole question see F. Schwenn (n. 63), 183f.

86. H. W. Parke and D. E. W. Wormell, *The Delphic Oracle*, Vol. 1, 1956, 295ff. (260): 'For the dramatic purposes of folk memory the command to offer a human sacrifice was the most thrilling answer the oracle could give.' Cf. Libanius, *Declamatio* 42.25 (7,415): οὐκ ἀκούετε τὸν Πύθιον . . .; καὶ οἱ μὲν παῖδες ἐτέθυντο.

87. Cf. e.g. the report by Caesar on the religion of the Gauls, *Bellum Gallicum* 6.16: 'The whole Gallic people is remarkably addicted to religious observances. So people suffering from severe illnesses or those who pass their lives in war and danger offer or vow to offer human sacrifices and employ Druids to perform the sacrificial rites. For they believe that unless the life of man be offered for man's life, the divine spirit cannot be propitiated (*quod pro vita hominis nisi hominis vita reddatur, non posse deorum immortalium numen placari*).' The whole account is biassed, in order to stress the barbarism of the Gauls. On the other hand, Caesar himself killed men 'as a sort of ritual observance' during a mutiny, Dio Cassius 43.24.3, see F. Schwenn, op. cit. (n. 63), 166f.

88. 8.9.4–12 (10): *Sicut caelo missus piaculum omnis deorum irae, qui pestem ab suis aversam in hostes ferret*, cf. Cicero, *De divinatione* 1.51, and the commentary by A. S. Pease, 184f.; *De finibus* 2.61; *De natura deorum* 2.10; 3.15, see above, p. 14. See also F. Schwenn, op. cit., 154ff.; W. Burkert, *Structure* (n. 63), 59–64. For the term *piaculum* see P. C. Tromp, *De Romanorum piaculis*, cf. 21.

89. Livy, 10.28.13: *datum hoc nostro generi est ut luendis periculis publicis piacula simus. iam ego mecum hostium legiones mactandas Telluri ac deis Manibus dabo.'* Cf. also Livy 8.10.12. For the frequent mention of the Decii in the Roman collections of *exempla virtutis* see H. W. Litchfield (n. 49), 48 n. 4. It extends as far as Dante, *Paradise* 6.47.

90. *Pharsalia* 2.304–9:
  Sic eat: inmites Romana piacula divi
  Plena ferant, nullo fraudemus sanguine bellum.
  Utinam caelique deis Erebique liceret
  Hoc caput in cunctas damnatum exponere poenas
  Devotum hostiles Decium, pressere catervae
  Me geminae figant acies, me barbara telis
  Rheni turba petat, cunctis ego pervius hostis
  Excipiam medius totius volnera belli.
  Hic redimat sanguis populos, hac caede luatur
  Quidquid Romani meruerunt pendere mores.
Cf. W. Speyer (n. 63), 139, who rightly points out that here 'the archaic thought pattern is ethicized'. I.e. the wrath of the gods, punishment and expiation here relate to moral guilt.

91. J. G. Frazer, *The Golden Bough*, Part VI, *The Scapegoat*, ³1925, gives a global survey of the theme of the scapegoat; for the *pharmakos* in Greece see 253ff. Cf. also F. Schwenn (n. 63), 26ff.; V. Gebhard, *Die Pharmakoi in Ionien und die Sybakchoi in Athen*, Munich dissertation 1926; id., 'Thargelia', *PW*, 2.R., 5, 1290–1304; id., 'Pharmakos', *PW* 19, 1841f.; M. P. Nilsson (n. 70) 1, 107ff.; L. Deubner, *Attische Feste*, ²1966 (1932), 179–88; G. Stählin, περίψημα, *TDNT* 6; W. Burkert, *Griechische Religion* (n. 63), 139ff.; *Structure* (n. 63), ch. III, 'Transformations of the Scapegoat', 59–77, 168ff. (with bibliography).

92. FGrHist 334, fr. 50 = Harpokration/Suda s.v.; cf. Helladios in Photius, *Bibliotheca*, p. 534 a3.

93. See Deubner (n. 91), 184 n. 5: Scholion Aristophanes, *Equites* 1136: λίαν ἀγεννεῖς καὶ ἀχρήστους ... ἔθυον; *Ranes* 730: τοὺς γὰρ φαύλους καὶ παρὰ τῆς φύσεως ἐπιβουλευομένους. ... ἔθυον. Cf. also scholion Aeschylus, *Septem contra Thebas* 680, Dindorf p. 376, 29: λιμοῦ συμβάντος παρ᾽ Ἕλλησιν ἢ τινος ἄλλου τῶν ἀπευκτῶν, λαμβάνοντες τὸν ἀηδέστατον, καὶ παρὰ τῆς φύσεως ἐπιβεβουλευομένον πηρόν, χωλόν, τοὺς τοιούτους, τοῦτον ἔθυον εἰς ἀπαλλαγὴν τοῦ ἐνοχλοῦντος δαίμονος.

94. See Deubner (n. 91), 186 n. 3 and 186 n. 2: Petronius according to Servius on Virgil, *Aeneid* 3,57 (= *Satyricon*, ed Konrad Müller, F1, p. 185) on Massilia: '*unus se ex pauperibus offerebat* ... *hic postea ornatus verbenis et vestibus sacris circumducebatur per totam civitatem cum execrationibus.*' Cf. Lactantius Placitus on Statius, *Thebaid* 10,793: he calls this form 'of purifying a city by human sacrifice a Gallic custom' (*lustrare civitatem humana hostia Gallicus mos est*), presumably because of the Celtic predilection for human sacrifice (see above, p. 87 n. 87). A very poor man (*aliquis de egentissimis*) was persuaded into selling himself for a high price: for a whole year he was fed on the choicest food.

On an appointed festival he was eventually led out of the city by the whole population and stoned by the people outside the city walls (*denique certo et solemni die per totam civitatem ductus ex urbe extra pomeria saxis occidebatus a populo*).

95. Strabo 10, 2, 9, C 452; cf. Ovid, *Fasti* 5, 629f. and the commentary by F. Bömer, 2, 330.

96. *P. Ovidii Nasonis Ibis*, ed. R. Ellis, Oxford 1881, p. 81. I owe this reference to Eberhard Jüngel. Cf. also the commentary, 140f.

97. Callimachus, ed. R. Pfeiffer, Oxford ²1965, I, 97: εἶτ' ἔξω τοῦ τείχους περίεισι κύκλῳ περικαθαίρων (?) αὐτῷ τὴν πόλιν, καὶ τότε ὑπὸ τοῦ βασιλέως καὶ τῶν ἄλλων λιθοβολεῖται, ἕως ἐξελασθῇ τῶν ὁρίων.

98. *Historiarum Variarum Chiliades*, ed. T. Kiessling, Leipzig 1826, 5, 729, 731. Cf. Deubner (n. 91), 183 n. 3. The treatment of the body corresponds with the action of the Trojans over the Locrian maiden whom they had killed, see W. Leaf, *Troy. A Study in Homeric Geography*, London 1912, 126ff. (129), 392ff.

99. *Acta Sanctorum Novembris* I, 1887, chs. 2–8, 106–8 (ch. 5 p. 107). On this cf. S. Weinstock, 'Saturnalien und Neujahrsfest in den Märtyreracten', in *Mullus, Festschrift T. Klauser*, Münster 1964, 391–400.

100. G. Stählin (n. 91).

101. J.-P. Vernant in J.-P. Vernant and P. Vidal-Naquet, *Mythe et tragédie en Grèce ancienne*, 1973, 117ff. (122): '*Roi divin-pharmakos*: telles sont donc les deux faces d'Oedipe, qui lui confèrent son aspect d'énigme en réunissant en lui, comme dans une formule à double sens, deux figures inverses l'une de l'autre. Cf. *Oedipus Rex* 1424ff.

102. *Oedipus Coloneus*, 1656–66.

103. Ibid. 1751:
                           ἐν οἷς γὰρ
            χάρις ἡ χθονία νὺξ ἀπόκειται
            πενθεῖν οὐ χρή.
cf. 1720: ἀλλ' ἐπεὶ ὀλβίως γ'ἔλυσεν
           τὸ τέλος, ὦ φίλαι, βίου.

104. Plutarch, *Pelopidas* 21 and 22, ET, LCL V,391ff., cf. Xenophon, *Hellenica* 6.4.7; Diodore 15.54.1–4; Pausanias 9.13.5f.: 'At that time Epaminondas sacrificed to Skedasos and his daughters and prayed that the battle should not take place to bring about the salvation of Thebans, but to wreak vengeance on them (the Spartans).' For the development of the saga of the Leuctrides Korai see F. Pfister, 'Skedasos', *PW* 2 R. 3, cols. 465ff.

105. For early Christianity as a 'mad superstition', see M. Hengel, *Crucifixion*, London and Philadelphia 1977, 1ff.

Chapter Two

1. W. Popkes, *Christus Traditus*, 1967, makes an excellent investigation of these 'surrender formulae', though I cannot follow his results at every point.

2. Here I can refer above all to the numerous works by J. Jeremias, see e.g. *Abba*, 1966; *New Testament Theology* Vol. 1, *The Proclamation of Jesus*, ET 1971, 286ff., 295ff.; cf. L. Goppelt, *Theologie des Neuen Testaments*, 1975, 1, 243ff.

3. *Weil Ich dich liebe. Die Verkündigung Jesu und Deuterojesaja*, 1976, 231ff.

4. On Mark 10.45 see now P. Stuhlmacher, 'Existenzvertretung für die Vielen: Mk 10.45 (Matt. 20, 28)', in *Werden und Wirken des Alten Testaments, Festschrift für Claus Westermann zum 70. Geburtstag*, 1980, 412–27. He rightly derives the logion from Jesus himself, see p. 95 n.55 below.

5. On this see W. Kramer, *Christ, Lord, Son of God*, ET SBT 50, London 1966, 26ff., 133ff. This is rightly corrected by K. Wengst (see above p. 76 n.4), 78ff. The term 'dying formula' also appears there.

6. The same is true of I Peter 2.21. The fact that I Peter prefers the verb πάσχειν to ἀποθνήσκειν is connected with his paraenetic application of the death of Jesus. Possibly he replaced ἀποθνήσκειν by πάσχειν in one of the passages that he incorporated.

7. Suetonius, *Claudius*, 25; in Tacitus, *Annals* 15, 44, 21 the reading should be *Chrestiani*. Cf. K. Weiss, *TDNT* 9, 484,35ff. and A. Wlosok, *Rom und die Christen*, 1970, 8–12.

8. On this see P. Stuhlmacher and K. Haacker et al., in *Biblisch-Theologische Studien* 1, 1977, 38f.

9. For the 'apostolic council' see my *Acts and the History of Earliest Christianity*, 1979, 111ff.

10. Op. cit., 71ff.; cf. 'Zwischen Jesus und Paulus. Die "Hellenisten", die "Sieben" und Stephanus (Apg 6,1–15; 7,54–8,3)', *ZThK* 72, 1975, 151–206 (literature).

11. It is the special contribution of the great commentary by R. Pesch, *Das Markusevangelium* II, 1977, that he investigates the historical background and here comes up against the towering significance of the question of the Messiah.

12. 'Der gekreuzigte Messias', in *Der historische Jesus und der kerygmatische Christus*, ed. H. Ristow and K. Matthiae, 1961, 161.

13. M. Hengel, *ZThK* 72, 1975, 192 n. 128; so also P. Stuhlmacher, *Das Evangelium von der Versöhnung in Christus*, 1979, 25f.

14. Op. cit., 23.

15. GenR. 65.22. See above, pp. 8f. Cf. M. Hengel, *Crucifixion*, 84f.

16. *JTS* 14, 1945, 4; see now also H. Gese (n. 11), *Die Sühne*, 85–106, esp. 105; P. Stuhlmacher, 'Zur neueren Exegese von Röm 3,24–26', in *Jesus und Paulus. Festschrift W. G. Kümmel zum 70. Geburtstag*, 1975, 314–33. The Tübingen dissertation by B. Janowski, *Sühne als Heilsgeschehen. Studien zur Sühnetheologie der Priesterschrift und zur Wurzel KPR im Alten Orient und im Alten Testament*, 1979, supervised by my colleague Hartmut Gese, is now of fundamental importance for the Old Testament concept of atonement. There is an investigation of Romans 3.25 in the light of underlying tradition in Part IV, 3B (pp. 242ff.).

17. In my study *Nachfolge und Charisma*, 1968, I have attempted to show that this designation is in no way sufficient.

18. The fundamental problem of chronology has not been taken seriously enough in connection with the question of the origin of christology; see my article 'Christologie und neutestamentliche Chronologie', in *Neues Testament und Geschichte, Festschrift O. Cullmann zum 70. Geburtstag*, 1972, 43–67.

19. See the extensive collection of evidence in W. Popkes, op. cit. (n. 1), 61ff. and 56 n. 1.

20. See above, p. 90, notes 3 and 4.

21. The penetrating linguistic analyses by J. Jeremias, *The Eucharistic Words of Jesus*, ET ²1966, 178ff., 225ff., 227 n. 5, are still of fundamental importance. The rare verbal correspondence of the two Targums points to the antiquity of this interpretation: *uzᵉraq 'al madbᵉḥā lᵉkappārā 'al 'ammā*. The rabbinic texts (other than the Targums) interpret Ex. 24.8 in terms of blood from circumcision, thus reducing the significance of atonement, in order to stand apart from Christianity. The two statements about atonement give the impression of being early relics.

22. Josephus, *Antt.* 20.200ff.: τὸν ἀδελφὸν Ἰησοῦ τοῦ λεγομένου Χριστοῦ, Ἰάκωβος ὄνομα αὐτῷ, καί τινας ἑτέρους, ὡς παρανομησάντων κατηγορίαν ποιησάμενος παρέδωκε λευσθησομένους. For Peter and James cf. Hengel, *Acts and the History of Earliest Christianity*, London and Philadelphia 1979, 92–98.

23. Epiphanius, *Panarion* 30, 16, 5–7: ἦλθον καταλῦσαι τὰς θυσίας, καὶ ἐὰν μὴ παύσησθε τοῦ θύειν, οὐ παύσεται ἀφ'ὑμῶν ἡ ὀργή. Cf. 19, 3, 6 (see A. F. J. Klijn and G. J. Reinink, *Patristic Evidence for Jewish-Christian Sects*, 1973, 182ff.).

24. *Recognitions* 1.35ff. There are further instances from the *Kerygmata Petrou* in G. Strecker, *Das Judenchristentum in den Pseudoklementinen*, 1958, 179ff. However, the criticism of sacrifice cannot be derived directly from a Jewish criticism; it is a rationalistic development of the attitude of the primitive community. In addition, we should assume Gnostic influence.

25. H. J. Schoeps, *Theologie und Geschichte des Judenchristentums* 1949, 219ff.: for the Ebionite hostility to the cult and their place in the history of religion, cf. *Das Judenchristentum*, 1964, 68ff., 95ff. Anti-Paulinism and then Gnostic influence may be responsible for the relative silence of the later Ebionite texts, since the gnostics were no longer interested in the death of Jesus. According to Jerome (*in Jes.* 31.6–9 = CC 73.404 = Klijn/Reinink, op. cit., 222f.), they took a positive attitude to God's mercy and the power of the cross, cf. also Epiphanius, *Panarion* 30.3.5, op. cit., 178, and Jerome, *Ep.* 112.13, op. cit., 200. They also had to deal with Deut. 21.23 (Jerome, *in Gal.*, MPL 26.387B = op.cit., 204).

26. Josephus, *Antt.* 18.19. On this see G. Klinzing, *Die Umdeutung des Kultus in der Qumrangemeinde und im NT*, 1971, 45ff.: 'The sending of gifts for dedication is the least binding way of honouring the Temple and does not amount to taking part in its cult.'

27. Eusebius, *HE* 2.23.6: μόνος εἰσήρχετο εἰς τὸν ναόν ... ἀεὶ κάμπτειν ἐπὶ γόνυ προσκυνοῦντα τῷ θεῷ καὶ αἰτεῖσθαι ἄφεσιν τῷ λαῷ.

28. On Isaiah 53 and the death of Jesus see the survey of research in M.-L. Gubler (p. 76, n. 2), 259–335.

29. See the well-considered verdict by W. Popkes (p. 81, n. 38), 47ff. (55): 'TestB 3,8 could be the point of connection between Isaiah 53 (attested as the LXX understands it) and the early New Testament, if it could be demonstrated that there was an interpretation of the servant songs in terms of a suffering Messiah in a group standing near to primitive Christianity. However, this cannot be taken as certain.' Only the discovery of a new text could help us out of this dilemma.

30. Cf. O. Cullmann, *Christology of the New Testament*, 111: 'We must not forget that at this time Judaism had by no means a single *fixed* concept of the Messiah' (author's italics, not reproduced in ET). He is followed by H. R. Balz, *Methodische Probleme der neutestamentlichen Christologie*, 1967, 112.

31. For LXX see K. F. Euler, *Die Verkündigung vom leidenden Gottesknecht aus Jes. 53 in der griechischen Bibel*, 1934. For the later translations and the Targum on the prophets see H. Hegermann, *Jesaja 53 in Hexapla, Targum und Peschitta*, 1954. For the rabbinate see G. Dalman, *Der leidende und der Sterbende Messias der Synagoge im ersten nachchristlichen Jahrtausend*, 1888; Billerbeck 1.481ff.; J. Jeremias, παῖς θεοῦ, *TDNT* 5, 677–700.

32. *RB* 70, 1963, 492.

33. The attack made on J. Jeremias with more vigour than critical understanding by M. Rese, 'Überprüfung einiger Thesen von J. Jeremias', *ZThK* 60, 1963, 21–41, goes to the opposite extreme, by funda-

mentally challenging any pre-Christian messianic interpretation. The fact that we have very few 'pre-Christian' messianic texts at all, and the problem of dating rabbinic haggadic traditions, which usually raise almost insuperable difficulties for us, is unknown to him. His interpretation of TestB 3,8 in terms of the 'death of the righteous', 24–8, is unsatisfactory. The completely sinless and perfect righteous one is the Messiah, see PsSol. 17. Unfortunately he does not go into the problem of the text of the LXX, which presents an amazing, background paraphrase.

34. A new investigation is urgently needed. The brief study by H. W. Wolff, *Jesaja 53*, ²1950, is still very well worth reading, although it shows its age. Cf. also J. Jeremias (n. 21), 191–216.

35. W. Popkes (p. 81, n. 38) goes into the relationship of the 'surrender' statements to Isa. 53, 219ff., 253ff., 258ff., but underestimates its significance.

36. *Novum Testamentum Graece*, ²⁶1979, 761.

37. For this theory by Wengst, which found a large degree of assent, see p. 3 above and M.-L. Gubler (p. 73, n. 2), 254ff., 316ff.

38. In this dating I am following E. Bickerman, *Studies in Jewish and Christian History* I, 1976, 276–81. The most recent investigation by K. Breitenstein, *Beobachtungen zu Sprache, Stil und Gedankengut des 4.Makkabäerbuchs*, 1976, follows A. Dupont-Sommer in assuming for linguistic reasons that the work was composed in the second half of the century. It is probable that IV Maccabees already presupposes the persecution of the Jews after AD 66–70, or even 115–117 and 132–136. The martyr story also found its way into the rabbinic tradition, see Gittin 57b; Lam.R. 1.50; Seder Eliyahu R. 30 (28).

39. Dan. 3.25–45. Cf. O. Plöger, 'Zusätze zu Daniel', *JSHRZ* I,1,67f.

40. Cf. Dan. 3.34 LXX with Job 42.8–10 (a) καὶ ἔλυσεν τὴν ἁμαρτίαν αὐτοῖς διὰ Ἰώβ and 11QtgJob (ed. J.P.M.v.d.Ploeg/A.S.v.d.Woude, 1971), col. 38,2f.: *wšbq lhwn ḥṭ'yhwn bdylh* (= Job). The Hebrew text mentions only Job's prayer for his friends.

41. The reading varies here between Theodotion and o¹ text καὶ ἐκτελέσαι ὄπισθέν σου is read by Theodotion and syʰ. In individual instances in LXX, ὀπίσω can stand for '*im* or *lipnē*: I Kings 1.8; I Sam. 17.31 and above all Dan. 8.4 (LXX).

42. On this see S. Spiegel, *The Last Trial*, 1963; G. Vermes, *Scripture and Tradition in Judaism*, ²1973, 193–227; R. J. Daly, 'The Soteriological Significance of the Sacrifice of Isaac', *CBQ* 39, 1977, 45–75; this is supplemented by P. R. Davies and B. D. Chilton, 'The Aqedah: A Revised Tradition History', *CBQ* 40, 1978, 514–46, though they 'under-interpret' the texts. Does the fact that haggadic parallels to the Targums first appear among the Amoreans really mean that the Targumic tradi-

tions are similarly as late? One cannot in any way conclude from the fact that we have little demonstrable 'Tannaitic Haggadah' that the Pharisaic teachers of the first and second centuries AD were relatively uninterested in the Haggadah. The Haggadah was often handed on anonymously. The wall-paintings of the synagogue of Dura Europos, for example, show how rich and living the Haggadah must have been even at the beginning of the third century AD. It goes back to earlier acknowledged traditions.

43. *LAB* 32,3 (ed. G. Kisch, p. 204): '*Erit autem mea beatitudo super omnes homines quia non erit aliud (sc. sacrificium), et in me annunciabunt generationes et per me intelligent populi, quoniam dignificavit Dominus animam hominis in sacrificium.*' For the interpretation of this difficult passage see P. R. Davies and B. D. Chilton (n. 42), 523ff.

44. 40.2–4 (G. Kisch, p. 220f.): '*Et nunc detur anima eius in peticione eius, et erit mors eius preciosa ante conspectum meum omni tempore*' (40.4). As in Euripides the voluntary nature of the sacrifice is stressed. The daughter consoles her despairing father: '*Et quis est qui contristetur moriens, videns populum liberatum?*' At the same time she points to the example of Isaac: '*et erat qui offerebatur paratus et qui offerebat gaudens.*' For the voluntary nature of the sacrifice of Isaac see e.g. GenR 56.8.

45. 18.5 (G. Kisch, p. 159): '*et filium eius petii in holocaustum et adduxit eum ut poneretur in sacrario, ego autem reddidi eum patri suo, et quia non contradixit (sc. Isaac), facta est oblatio in conspectu meo acceptabilis, et pro sanguine eius elegi istos.*' R. Le Déaut, *La nuit pascale*, 1963, 158, and Davies and Chilton are wrong in supposing that the passage can be referred to Abraham.

46. Mek. de R. Yishmael on Ex. 12.23 (Lauterbach 1,87): 'Another interpretation. "And when he (Yahweh) sees the blood." ' He sees the blood of the '*aqedat* of Isaac, as is said: 'and Abraham called the place "Yahweh will see" ' (Gen. 22.14). The anonymous interpretation points to an earlier tradition (against P. R. Davies and B. D. Chilton, 536). In the Haggadah there is no 'normative interpretation' in the strict sense, as there is in the Halachah. One cannot draw the conclusion from the introduction that this must be an early tradition. It is a traditional interpretation which has become anonymous. For the age of the Mekilta de R. Yishmael see now G. Stemberger, *Kairos* 21, 1979, 84–118.

47. *Märtyrer und Gottesknecht*, ²1963.

48. *Die Aggada der Tannaiten* I, ²1903, 1–72 (including the pupils of Johanan ben Zakkai). Cf. also the critical view of J. Neusner, *The Rabbinic Traditions about the Pharisees before 70*, I–III, 1971.

49. jSanh 11,7,30c, lines 29ff.: '*wth htyph šyṣ't m'wtw ṣdyq kyprh 'l kl ysr'l.*

50. §333 (ed. Finkelstein, p. 383, 6).

51. Pishā c.1, lines 106f. (Lauterbach 1,10): *šh'bwt whnby'ym ntnw npšm 'l ysr'l*, with reference to Moses' offer to atone in Ex. 32.32. Cf. lines 111ff. (p. 1,11).

52. Sifre Num. 25.13 §139 (Horovitz, p. 173,16f.). See M. Hengel, *Die Zeloten*, ²1976, 161f.

53. MSanh 2.1f. par TSanh 4.1 (Zuckermandel), p. 420: TShebuot 1.4 (446 par.); Sifre Num. 35.24 §161 (Horovitz p. 222,5), cf. also MNeg 2,1.

54. Op. cit., (n.47), 63ff.

55. Text following W. Staerk, *Altjüdische liturgische Gebete*, KlT 58, ²1930, Palestinian recension. Second petition: the twofold *mᵉhayyeh ham-metim* also appears alongside it. Cf. Paul (a) with finite verb (ἤγειρεν): Rom. 10.9; I Cor. 6.14; cf. I Thess. 1.10; I Cor. 15.14. (b) With the aorist participle (ἐγείρας as a predicate of God): Rom. 4.24; 8.11; II Cor. 1.9; 4.14; Gal. 1.1; Eph. 1.20; Col. 2.12; Acts only with the finite verb: 3.15; 4.10; 5.30; 13.30, 37; I Peter, aorist participle: 1.21. See also P. Stuhlmacher, 'Auferweckung Jesu und Biblische Theologie', *ZThK* 70, 1973, 365–403 (387).

56. For all its interesting observations, the main thesis of Klaus Berger, *Die Auferstehung des Propheten und die Erhöhung des Menschensohnes*, 1976, is unconvincing, despite its wealth of material and valuable insights. See the objections made by E. Schweizer, *TLZ* 103, 1978, 874–8, and my controversy with R. Pesch, who refers to Berger's theories, *ThQ* 153, 1973, 252–69.

57. The interpretation of this, the most important christological text in the Old Testament after Isa. 53 in terms of the risen Son of Man, was similarly made in the earliest community, as is shown by the prayer *mārān 'ᵃtā* (I Cor. 16.22), see my study 'Hymnus und Christologie', in *Festschrift K.H. Rengstorf zum 75. Geburtstag*, 1980, 1–23, see also D. M. Hay, *Glory at the Right Hand*, 1973, and M. Gourgues, *A la droite de Dieu*, Paris 1980.

58. Against M. Dibelius, *Studies in the Acts of the Apostles*, 1956, 124: 'A band of people had been gathered together in a common belief in Jesus Christ and in the expectation of his coming again, and were leading a quiet, and in the Jewish sense,"pious" existence in Jerusalem. It was a modest existence,and nothing but the victorious conviction of the believers betrayed the fact that from this company a movement would go out which was to change the world.' He is followed by E. Haenchen, *The Acts of the Apostles*, 1971, 189: 'It is likely, however, that in reality the Christians sought adherents for their Lord, in the earliest days, without attracting much attention . . . it was the "Hellenists" who first broke out from this reserve of the Jewish sect that believed

in Jesus.' This is to underestimate the power of eschatological enthusiasm; the first Christians did not expect less than happened later, but infinitely more, namely the complete transformation of the world by the return of the crucified Jesus. The missionary impulse which this provided is shown not least in the winning over of the Hellenists. See 'Die Ursprünge der christlichen Mission', *NTS* 18, 1971/72, 30ff.

59. M. Hengel, 'Maria Magdalena und die Frauen als Zeugen', in *Abraham Unser Vater, Festschrift O. Michel z. 60. Geburtstag*, Leiden 1963, 253.

60. Lauterbach 2,290.

61. See Walter Bauer, *Das Leben Jesu im Zeitalter der neutestamentlichen Apokryphen*, 1909 (reprinted 1967), 467, cf. *C.Cels*. 2.9, 10, 12, 18; 6.10; A. von Harnack, *Der Philosoph bei Makarius Magnes, Kritik des Neuen Testaments von einem griechischen Philosophen des 3. Jhs.*, TU 37,4, p. 34 (3,2).

62. See the fine investigation by H. Schürmann, *Jesu ureigener Tod*, ²1975.

63. *The Eucharistic Words of Jesus*, ²1966; *New Testament Theology I, The Proclamation of Jesus*, 1971, 277ff., 288ff. Cf. also, with a partly different emphasis, H. Patsch, *Abendmahl und historischer Jesus*, 1972, and L. Goppelt, *Theologie des Neuen Testaments I, Jesu Wirken in seiner theologischen Bedeutung*, 1975, 234ff., 241ff., 261ff.

64. For the eucharist as a death meal see H. Gese, *Zur biblischen Theologie*, 1977, 107–27: the origin of the Lord's Supper, which already gives this character to the last meal of Jesus with his disciples.

65. See *The Son of God*, ET 1976, 89ff. For the Philippians hymn see O. Hofius, *Der Christushymnus Philipper 2, 6–11*, 1976.

66. For the Near Eastern and Old Testament background to atonement and its different modes of theological interpretation, see the excellent dissertation by B. Janowski, *Sühne als Heilsgeschehen*, Tübingen Dissertation 1979, which will soon be published in WMANT.

BIBLIOGRAPHY

On Chapter 1

Baumeister, T., *Die Anfänge der Theologie des Martyriums*, MBT 45, Münster 1980

Benz, E., *Das Todesproblem in der stoischen Philosophie*, TBAW 7, Stuttgart 1929

Betz, H. D. (ed.), *Plutarch's Theological Writings and Early Christian Literature*, SCHNT 3, Leiden 1975

Burkert, W., 'Greek Tragedy and Sacrificial Ritual', *GRBS* 7, 1966, 87–121

—, *Griechische Religion der archaischen und klassischen Epoche*, RM 15, Stuttgart 1977

—, *Homo necans. Interpretationen altgriechischer Opferriten und Mythen*, RVV 32, Berlin and New York 1972

—, *Structure and History in Greek Mythology and Ritual*, Berkeley 1979

Campenhausen, H. von, *Die Idee des Martyriums in der Alten Kirche*, Göttingen [2]1964

Detienne, M., and Vernant, J.-P., *La cuisine du sacrifice en pays grec*, Paris 1979

Deubner, L., *Attische Feste*, Hildesheim [2]1966 (reprint of 1932 edition)

—, 'Der Pharmakos von Abdera', *SIFC* NS 11, 1934, 185–92

Dodds, E. R., 'Euripides the Irrationalist', in *The Ancient Concept of Progress and Other Essays on Greek Literature and Belief*, Oxford 1973, 78–91

Eitrem, S., *Die göttlichen Zwillinge bei den Griechen*, SNVAO. HF, 1902, 2

Farnell, L. R., *Greek Hero Cults and Ideas of Immortality*, Oxford 1970 (reprint of 1921 edition)

Fraenkel, H., *Dichtung und Philosophie des frühen Griechentums*, Munich [3]1969

Frazer, J. G., *The Golden Bough. A Study in Magic and Religion*. Part VI: *The Scapegoat*, London [3]1925

Gebhard, V., *Die Pharmakoi in Ionien und die Sybakchoi in Athen*, Munich dissertation 1926

Gese, H., 'Der Messias', *Zur biblischen Theologie*, Munich 1977, 128–51

—, 'Die Sühne', op. cit., 85–106

—, 'Der Tod im Alten Testament', op. cit., 31–54

Girard, R., *La violence et le sacré*, Paris 1972

Gnilka, J., 'Martyriumsparänese und Sühnetod in synoptischen und jüdischen Traditionen', in *Die Kirche des Anfangs, Festschrift H. Schürmann*, Leipzig 1977; ETS 38, Freiburg 1978, 223–46

Gubler, M-L., *Die frühesten Deutungen des Todes Jesu*, OBO 15, Fribourg and Göttingen 1977

Hengel, M., *Crucifixion in the Ancient World and the Folly of the Message of the Cross*, London and Philadelphia 1977

—, *Jews, Greeks and Barbarians*, London and Philadelphia 1980

—, *Judaism and Hellenism*, London and Philadelphia 1974

—, *Die Zeloten*, AGJU 1, Leiden ²1976

Hommel, H., 'Dulce et decorum . . .', *RhMus* 111, 1968, 219–52

Kaiser, O., 'Den Erstgeboren deiner Söhne sollst du mir geben', in *Denkender Glaube, Festschrift C.H. Ratschow zum 65*, Berlin 1976, 24–48.

Kellermann, U., *Auferstanden in den Himmel*, SBS 95, Stuttgart 1979

Koch, K., 'Sühne und Sündenvergebung um die Wende von der exilischen zur nachexilischen Zeit', *EvTh* 26, 1966, 217–39

Kümmel, H.M., 'Ersatzkönig und Sündenbock', *ZAW* 80, 1968, 289-318

Lasaulx, E. von, *Die Sühnopfer der Griechen und Römer und ihr Verhältnis zu dem Einen auf Golgatha*, Würzburg 1841

Latte, K., *Römische Religionsgeschichte*, HAW 5, 4, Munich ²1967

Litchfield, H. W., 'National *Exempla Virtutis* in Roman Literature', *HSCP* 25, 1914, 1–71

Lohfink, G., *Die Himmelfahrt Jesu*, SANT 26, Munich 1971

Muehl, M., 'Des Herakles Himmelfahrt', *RhMus* 101, 1958, 106–34

Mommsen, T., *Römisches Strafrecht*, Darmstadt 1955 (reprint of 1899 edition)

Musurillo, H. A., *The Acts of the Pagan Martyrs. Acta Alexandrinorum*, Oxford 1954)

Nilsson, M. P., *Geschichte der Griechischen Religion*, HAW 5, 2, Munich I, ²1961; II, ²1965

—, *Griechische Feste von religiöser Bedeutung*, Darmstadt 1957 (reprint of 1906 edition)

Oltramare, H., *Les origines de la diatribe romaine*, Geneva 1926

Parke, H. W., and Wormell, D. E. W., *The Delphic Oracle*, Oxford 1958

Pfister, F., 'Herakles und Christus', *ARW* 34, 1937, 42–60

Popkes, W., *Christus traditus*, ATANT 49, Zurich and Stuttgart 1967

Robinson, P. A., *The Conception of Death in Judaism in the Hellenistic and Early Roman Period*, London 1980

Rose, H. J., 'Herakles and the Gospels', *HTR* 31, 1938, 113–42

Roussel, P., 'Le thème du sacrifice volontaire dans la tragédie d'Euripide', *RBPH* 1, 1922, 225–40

Ruppert, L., *Jesus als der leidende Gerechte?*, SBS 59, Stuttgart 1972
—, *Der leidende Gerechte*, Würzburg and Stuttgart 1972

Schmitt, J., *Freiwilliger Opfertod bei Euripides*, RVV 17, 2, Giessen 1921

Schwartz, E., *Ethik der Griechen*, Stuttgart 1951

Schwenn, F., *Die Menschenopfer bei den Griechen und Römern*, RVV 15, 3, Giessen 1915

Simon, M., *Hercule et le christianisme*, PFLUS, Second Series, 19, Paris 1955

Speyer, W., 'Religionen des griechisch-römischen Bereichs. Zorn der Gottheit, Vergeltung und Sühne', in *Theologie und Religionswissenschaft*, ed U. Mann, Darmstadt 1973, 124-43

Steck, O. H., *Israel und das gewaltsame Geschick der Propheten*, WMANT 23, Neukirchen-Vluyn 1967

Steinkopf, G., *Untersuchungen zur Geschichte des Ruhmes bei den Griechen*, Halle/Wittenberg dissertation 1937

Stengel, P., *Opferbräuche der Griechen*, Darmstadt 1972 (reprint of 1910 edition)

Tromp, S. P. C., *De Romanorum Piaculis*, Lugduni Batavorum dissertation 1921

Vernant, J.-P., and Vidal-Naquet, P., *Mythe et tragédie en Grèce ancienne*, Paris 1972

Waechter, L., *Der Tod im Alten Testament*, AzTh, Second Series 8, Stuttgart 1967

Wengst, L., *Christologische Formeln und Lieder des Urchristentums*, StNT 7, Gütersloh ²1973

Wilamowitz-Moellendorff, U. von, *Der Glaube der Hellenen*, Darmstadt ²1955

Yerkes, R. K., *Sacrifice in Greek and Roman Religions and Early Judaism*, New York 1952

On Chapter 2

Bacher, W., *Die Aggada der Tannaiten*, Strassburg, I, ²1903

Balz, H. R., *Methodische Probleme der neutestamentlichen Christologie*, WMANT 25, Neukirchen-Vluyn 1967

Barrett, C. K., 'The Background of Mark 10.45', in *New Testament Essays. Studies in Memory of T. W. Manson*, edited by A. J. B. Higgins, London 1959, 1–18

Bauer, W., *Das Leben Jesu im Zeitalter der neutestamentlichen Apokryphen*, Darmstadt 1967 (reprint of 1909 edition)

Baumeister, T., *Die Anfänge der Theologie des Martyriums*, MBT 45, Munster 1980

Berger, K., *Die Auferstehung des Propheten und die Erhöhung des Menschensohnes*, SUNT 13, Göttingen 1976

Bickerman, E., *Studies in Jewish and Christian History*, AGJU 9, I, Leiden 1976

Breitenstein, K., *Beobachtungen zu Sprache, Stil und Gedankengut des 4. Makkabäerbuches*, Basle and Stuttgart 1976

Conzelmann, H., 'Historie und Theologie in den synoptischen Passionsberichten', in *Zur Bedeutung des Todes Jesu*, Gütersloh 1967, 35–53

—, 'Zur Analyse der Bekenntnisformel I. Kor. 15, 3–5', *EvTh* 25, 1965, 1–11

Cullmann, O., *The Christology of the New Testament*, London and Philadelphia ²1963

Dahl, N. A., 'The Atonement – An Adequate Reward for the Akedah? (Ro 8:32)', in *Neotestamentica et Semitica, Studies in Honour of M. Black*, edited by E. Ellis and M. Wilcox, Edinburgh 1969, 15–29

—, 'Der gekreuzigte Messias', in *Der historische Jesus und der kerygmatische Christus*, edited by H. Ristow and K. Matthiae, Berlin ²1962 149–69

Dalman, G., *Der leidende und der sterbende Messias der Synagoge im ersten nachchristlichen Jahrtausend*, SIJB 4, Leipzig 1888

Daly, R. J., 'The Soteriological Significance of the Sacrifice of Isaac', *CBQ* 39, 1977, 45–75

Davies, P. R., and Chilton, B. D., 'The Aqedah: A Revised Tradition History', *CBQ* 40, 1978, 514–46

Le Déaut, R., *La nuit pascale*, AnBib 22, Rome 1963

Delling, G., *Der Kreuzestod Jesu in der urchristlichen Verkündigung*, Göttingen 1972

Dibelius, M., 'The First Christian Historian', in *Studies in the Acts of the Apostles*, London 1956

Euler, K. F., *Die Verkündigung vom leidenden Gottesknecht aus Jes. 53 in der griechischen Bibel*, BWANT 66, Fourth Series, 14, Stuttgart 1934

Gese, H., 'Die Herkunft des Herrenmahls', in *Zur biblischen Theologie*, Munich 1977, 107–27

—, 'Psalm 22 und das Neue Testament', in *Vom Sinai zum Zion*, Munich 1974, 180–201

—, 'Die Sühne', in *Zur biblischen Theologie*, Munich 1977, 85–106

Goppelt, L., *Theologie des Neuen Testaments I, Jesu Wirken in seiner theologischen Bedeutung*, edited by J. Roloff, Göttingen 1975

Gourgues, M., *A la droite de Dieu*, Paris 1978

Grimm, W., *Weil Ich dich liebe. Die Verkündigung Jesu und Deuterojesaja*, ANTJ 1, Berne and Frankfurt 1976

Gubler, M.-L., *Die frühesten Deutungen des Todes Jesu*, OBO 15, Fribourg and Göttingen 1977

Haenchen, E., *The Acts of the Apostles*, Oxford and Philadelphia 1971

Hahn, F., *Christologische Hoheitstitel*, FRLANT 83, Göttingen 1963

Harnack, A. von, *Kritik des Neuen Testaments von einem griechischen Philosophen des 3. Jhs.*, TU 37, 4, Third Series 7, Leipzig 1911

Hay, D. M., *Glory at the Right Hand*, Nashville and New York 1973

Hegermann, H., *Jesaja 53 in Hexapla, Targum und Peschitta*, BFCT Second Series 56, Gütersloh 1954

Hengel, M., 'Christologie und neutestamentliche Chronologie', in *Neues Testament und Geschichte. Festschrift for O. Cullmann*, Zurich and Tübingen 1972, 43–67

—, 'Hymnus und Christologie', in *Festschrift K. H. Rengstorf zum 75. Geburtstag*, Leiden 1980, 1–23

—, 'Ist der Osterglaube noch zu retten?', *ThQ* 153, 252–69

—, *Nachfolge und Charisma*, Berlin 1968

—, *The Son of God*, London and Philadelphia 1976

—, 'Die Ursprünge der christlichen Mission', *NTS* 18, 1971/72, 15–38

—, *Die Zeloten*, AGJU 1, Leiden ²1976

—, *Acts and the History of Earliest Christianity*, London and Philadelphia 1979

—, 'Zwischen Jesus und Paulus. Die "Hellenisten", die "Sieben" und Stephanus (Apg 6,1–15; 7,54–8,3)', *ZTK* 72, 1975, 151–206

Hofius, O., *Der Christushymnus Philipper 2,6–11*, WUNT First Series 17, Tübingen 1976

Hooker, M. D., *Jesus and the Servant*, London 1959

Janowski, B., *Sühne als Heilsgeschehen*, Diss. Tübingen 1979

Jeremias, J., *Abba*, Göttingen 1966

Jeremias, J., *The Eucharistic Words of Jesus*, London and Philadelphia ²1966

—, 'Die älteste Schicht der Menschensohn-Logien', *ZNW* 58, 1966, 159–72

—, "Ἀμνὸς τοῦ θεοῦ-παῖς θεοῦ', *ZNW* 34, 1935, 115–23

—, 'Artikelloses Χριστός. Zur Ursprache von 1. Cor. 15,3b–5', *ZNW* 57, 1966, 211–15

—, 'Das Lösegeld für Viele (Mk 10,45), in *Abba*, Göttingen 1966, 216–99

—, *New Testament Theology Vol. 1: The Proclamation of Jesus*, London and New York 1971

—, 'παῖς θεοῦ', *TDNT* 5, 654–717

—, 'παῖς(θεοῦ) im Neuen Testament', in *Abba*, Göttingen 1966, 191–216

—, 'Zum Problem der Deutung von Jesaja 53 im palästinensischen Spätjudentum', in *Aux sources de la tradition chrétienne, Mélanges M. Goguel*, Neuchâtel and Paris 1950, 113–19

Käsemann, E., 'Die Heilsbedeutung des Todes Jesu nach Paulus', in *Zur Bedeutung des Todes Jesu*, Gütersloh ²1967, 11–34

Kessler, H., *Die theologische Bedeutung des Todes Jesu*, Düsseldorf 1970

Kilian, R., *Isaaks Opferung*, SBS 44, Stuttgart 1970

Klijn, A. F. J., and Reinink, G. J., *Patristic Evidence for Jewish-Christian Sects*, NT.S 36, Leiden 1973

Klinzing, G., *Die Umdeutung des Kultus in der Qumrangemeinde und im Neuen Testament*, SUNT 7, Göttingen 1971

Kramer, W., *Christ, Lord, Son of God*, SBT 50, London 1966

Leaf, W., *Troy. A Study in Homeric Geography*, London 1912

Lehmann, K., *Auferweckt am dritten Tag nach der Schrift*, QD 38, Freiburg 1968

Levi, I., 'Le sacrifice d'Isaac et la mort de Jésus', *REJ* 64, 1912, 161–84

—, 'Encore quelques mots sur le sacrifice d'Isaac', *REJ* 65, 1913, 138–43

Lindars, B., 'Passion Apologetic', in *New Testament Apologetic*, London 1961, 75–137

Lohse, E., 'Die alttestamentlichen Bezüge im neutestamentlichen Zeugnis vom Tode Jesu', in *Zur Bedeutung des Todes Jesu*, Gütersloh ²1967, 97–112

—, *Märtyrer und Gottesknecht*, FRLANT 64, New Series 46, Göttingen ²1963

Manson, T. W., "ΙΛΑΣΤΗΡΙΟΝ', *JTS* 46, 1945, 1–10

Morris, L., 'The Meaning of "ΙΛΑΣΤΗΡΙΟΝ in Romans III, 25', *NTS* 2, 1955, 33–43

Nauck, W., 'Freude im Leiden', *ZNW* 46, 1955, 68–80

Neusner, J., *The Rabbinic Traditions about the Pharisees before 70*, I–III, Leiden 1971

Patsch, H., *Abendmahl und historischer Jesus*, Stuttgart 1972

—, 'Zum alttestamentlichen Hintergrund von Röm 4,25 und 1.Ptr 2,24', *ZNW* 60, 1969, 273–9

Pesch, R., *Das Abendmahl und Jesu Todesverständnis*, QD 80, Freiburg 1978

—, *Das Markusevangelium* II, HTK 2,2, Freiburg 1978

—, *Wie Jesus das Abendmahl hielt*, Freiburg, Basle and Vienna 1977

Plöger, O., 'Zusätze zu Daniel', *JSHRZ* 1, 1973, 63–86

Popkes, W., *Christus traditus*, ATANT 49, Zürich and Stuttgart 1967

Rese, M., 'Überprüfung einiger Thesen von J. Jeremias zum Thema des Gottesknechtes im Judentum', *ZTK* 60, 1963, 21–41

Robinson, P. A., *The Conception of Death in Judaism in the Hellenistic and Early Roman Period*, London 1980

Roloff, J., 'Anfänge der soteriologischen Deutung des Todes Jesu', *NTS* 19, 1972, 38–64

Ruppert, L., *Jesus als der leidende Gerechte?*, SBS 59, Stuttgart 1972

Schoeps, H. J., *Das Judenchristentum*, Berne and Munich 1964

—, 'Die jüdischen Prophetenmorde', in *Aus frühchristlicher Zeit. Religionsgeschichtliche Untersuchungen*, Tübingen 1950, 126–43

—, *Paul. The Theology of the Apostle in the Light of Jewish Religious History*, London 1961

—, *Theologie und Geschichte des Judenchristentums*, Tübingen 1949

Schrage, W., 'Das Verständnis des Todes Jesu Christi im NT', in *Das Kreuz Jesu Christi als Grund des Heils*, edited by F. Viering, Gütersloh ²1968, 49–89

Schürmann, H., *Der Einsetzungsbericht Lk 22, 19–20*, NTA 20,4, Münster 1955

—, *Jesu Abschiedsrede Lk 22,21–38*, NTA 20,5, Münster 1957

—, *Jesu ureigener Tod*, Freiburg, Basle and Vienna 1975

—, 'Wie hat Jesus seinen Tod bestanden und verstanden?', in *Orientierung an Jesus, Festschrift J. Schmid*, edited by P. Hoffmann, Freiburg 1973, 325–63

Schwager, R., *Brauchen wir einen Sündenbock?*, Munich 1978

Schweizer, E., 'Das Abendmahl. Eine Vergegenwärtigung des Todes Jesu oder ein eschatologisches Freudenmahl?', *TZ* 2, 1946, 81–101

—, 'Besprechung von K. Berger, *Die Auferstehung des Propheten und die Erhöhung des Menschensohnes*', *TLZ* 103, 1978, cols. 874–8

—, *Erniedrigung und Erhöhung bei Jesus und seinen Nachfolgern*, ATANT 28, Zurich ²1962

Spiegel, S., *The Last Trial. Translated from the Hebrew with an introduction by J. Goldin*, New York 1967 (original in *Alexander Marx Jubilee Volume*, New York 1950)

Staerk, W., *Altjüdische liturgische Gebete*, KIT 58, Berlin ²1930

Starcky, J., 'Les quatre étapes du messianisme à Qumrân', *RB* 70, 1963, 481–505

Strecker, G., *Das Judenchristentum in den Pseudoklementinen*, TU 70, Fifth Series 15, Berlin 1958

Stuhlmacher, P., 'Das Bekenntnis zur Auferweckung Jesu von den Toten und die Biblische Theologie', *ZTK* 70, 1973, 365–403

—, and Class, H., *Das Evangelium von der Versöhnung in Christus*, Stuttgart 1979

—, 'Existenzstellvertretung für die Vielen: Mk 10,45 (Mt 20,28)', in *Werden und Wirken des Alten Testaments, Festschrift C. Westermann*, Göttingen and Neukirchen 1980, 412–27

—, 'Zum Thema: Biblische Theologie des Neuen Testaments', in *Biblisch-theologische Studien* 1, edited by K. Haacker and others, 1977, 25–60

—, 'Zur neueren Exegese von Röm 3,24–26', *Jesus und Paulus, Festschrift W. G. Kümmel*, Göttingen 1975, 315–33

Vermes, G., 'Redemption and Genesis XXII – The Binding of Isaac and the Sacrifice of Jesus', in *Scripture and Tradition in Judaism*, Haggadic Studies, StPB IV, Leiden 1961, ²1973, 193-227

Vielhauer, P., 'Gottesreich und Menschensohn in der Verkündigung Jesu', in *Festschrift Günther Dehn*, edited by W. Schneemelcher, 51–79; reprinted in *Aufsätze zum Neuen Testament*, Munich 1965, 55–91

Viering, F., *Der Kreuzestod Jesu. Interpretation eines theologischen Gutachtens*, Gütersloh 1969

Weiss, K., χρηστός, *TDNT* 9, 483–9

—, *Der leidende Gerechte und seine Feinde*, Würzburg 1973

Wengst, K., *Christologische Formeln und Lieder des Urchristentums*, StNT 7, Gütersloh ²1973

Whiteley, D. E. H., 'St Paul's Thoughts on the Atonement', *JTS* NS 8, 1957, 240–55

Wlosok, A., *Rom und die Christen*, Stuttgart 1970

Wolff, H. W., *Jesaja 53 im Urchristentum* Berlin ³1952

Wood, J. E., 'Isaac Typology in the New Testament', *NTS* 14, 1967/68, 583–9

INDEX OF BIBLICAL REFERENCES

INDEX OF ANCIENT AUTHORS

INDEX OF MODERN SCHOLARS